Husn Ara

I0004072

Table of Contents

Husn Ara

Chapter-1 Introduction to MLOps

What is MLOps?

MLOps (Machine Learning Operations) is a practice that applies the principles of DevOps to the machine learning lifecycle. It combines machine learning model development and operational processes to streamline the deployment, monitoring, and maintenance of machine learning models in production.

Key Components of MLOps:

1. **Collaboration Between Teams**: MLOps fosters collaboration between data scientists, machine learning engineers, and IT operations teams to ensure smooth model deployment.
2. **Automation**: It introduces automation into various phases of machine learning, such as data preparation, model training, testing, and deployment, to speed up the model development process and reduce human errors.
3. **Continuous Integration & Continuous Deployment (CI/CD)**: MLOps enables continuous integration of code, data, and machine learning models, followed by continuous deployment of new models into production systems.
4. **Monitoring & Maintenance**: MLOps includes real-time monitoring and logging for tracking model performance, detecting drift, and ensuring that models continue to perform well after deployment.
5. **Scalability**: MLOps provides the infrastructure and tools needed to scale machine learning projects, from development to large-scale deployment across multiple environments.

Benefits of MLOps:

- **Faster Deployment**: Automating model deployment significantly reduces time-to-market.
- **Better Model Performance**: Continuous monitoring and retraining ensure optimal model performance.
- **Increased Collaboration**: Promotes better communication between data science and engineering teams.
- **Improved Efficiency**: Reduces manual intervention and streamlines the entire machine learning lifecycle.

In short, MLOps integrates machine learning processes with DevOps best practices, enabling organizations to scale AI solutions efficiently and maintain models over time.

Importance of MLOps in the Machine Learning Lifecycle

MLOps (Machine Learning Operations) is critical for ensuring the success and scalability of machine learning projects. By integrating machine learning with operations, MLOps helps manage the complexities of the machine learning lifecycle—from model development to production deployment and maintenance. Here's why MLOps is essential:

1. Facilitates Collaboration Between Teams

MLOps promotes seamless collaboration between data scientists, machine learning engineers, and operations teams. It aligns efforts across various roles, ensuring that models developed by data scientists can be easily transitioned into production environments by engineers, with operational support for continuous monitoring and maintenance.

2. Streamlines Model Development and Deployment

The machine learning lifecycle involves multiple steps, including data collection, feature engineering, model training, validation, and deployment. MLOps automates many of these steps, allowing faster iterations in model development. This streamlining accelerates the time it takes to deploy machine learning models into production.

3. Ensures Reproducibility

One of the biggest challenges in machine learning is reproducibility—being able to recreate experiments and models reliably. MLOps standardizes processes like data versioning, experiment tracking, and model version control, ensuring that models can be reproduced consistently across different environments and team members.

4. Supports Continuous Integration and Continuous Deployment (CI/CD)

MLOps integrates CI/CD pipelines into the machine learning process. This means that new models, or updates to existing models, can be automatically tested and deployed into production environments without manual intervention. This leads to faster deployment cycles and reduces errors in the deployment process.

5. Automates Monitoring and Maintenance

Once a machine learning model is deployed, it requires ongoing monitoring to track its performance, detect drift (i.e., changes in data patterns), and ensure it meets business goals. MLOps automates the monitoring and logging of models, providing alerts when models degrade or when retraining is necessary. This ensures that models remain accurate and relevant over time.

6. Handles Model Retraining and Data Drift

As new data flows in, machine learning models might become less accurate due to changes in data distribution (a phenomenon known as data drift). MLOps provides mechanisms to automatically detect such changes and trigger model retraining, ensuring that the model remains effective as data evolves.

7. Enhances Scalability

MLOps provides the infrastructure and automation needed to scale machine learning efforts. It allows teams to build, deploy, and manage multiple models at once, accommodating growing datasets, increased model complexity, and a large number of use cases. This scalability is crucial for organizations that aim to deploy AI at scale.

8. Increases Model Reliability and Performance

MLOps ensures that models deployed in production are reliable, efficient, and scalable. Through performance monitoring and optimization, MLOps makes sure that the models deliver consistent results and adapt to changing requirements or data, leading to improved performance in real-world applications.

9. Ensures Compliance and Governance

With regulations such as GDPR and CCPA, managing machine learning projects within compliant frameworks is essential. MLOps provides the tools to track model versions, datasets, and logs, ensuring accountability, compliance, and data governance. It also supports transparency, which is crucial for auditing AI-driven decisions.

10. Reduces Operational and Maintenance Costs

By automating processes and reducing manual intervention, MLOps minimizes the operational overhead needed to maintain machine learning models. It reduces costs related to model monitoring, retraining, and redeployment by automating these processes, leading to a more efficient and cost-effective machine learning pipeline.

Conclusion

MLOps is essential in modern machine learning workflows as it streamlines the development, deployment, and maintenance of machine learning models. It brings operational rigor to machine learning, ensuring models are reproducible, scalable, and continuously improving. This is particularly important in large-scale AI deployments, where the ability to iterate quickly and maintain models over time is critical for success.

DevOps vs. MLOps: Key Differences

While DevOps and MLOps share common principles of collaboration, automation, and continuous delivery, they serve different purposes within software and machine learning environments. Here's a breakdown of the key differences between DevOps and MLOps:

1. Purpose and Focus

- **DevOps**: Focuses on automating and streamlining the software development lifecycle (SDLC) by improving collaboration between software development (Dev) and IT operations (Ops). The goal is to deliver software applications more quickly and reliably through continuous integration (CI), continuous delivery (CD), and infrastructure management.
- **MLOps**: Focuses on managing the machine learning lifecycle, which includes data collection, model development, deployment, monitoring, and retraining. MLOps applies DevOps principles to machine learning workflows to ensure the smooth deployment of models into production and their ongoing maintenance.

2. Artifacts and Lifecycle

- **DevOps Artifacts**: The primary artifact in DevOps is **software code**. The lifecycle involves coding, building, testing, and deploying software applications.
- **MLOps Artifacts**: In MLOps, the artifacts include **machine learning models**, **datasets**, and **training code**. The lifecycle is more complex and includes data ingestion, model training, model validation, deployment, and monitoring. It requires handling not only code but also data pipelines and model management.

3. Lifecycle Stages

- **DevOps Lifecycle**:
    - Plan
    - Code
    - Build
    - Test
    - Deploy
    - Operate
    - Monitor
- **MLOps Lifecycle**:
    - Data Collection and Preprocessing
    - Model Training and Experimentation
    - Model Validation
    - Model Deployment
    - Model Monitoring and Retraining
    - Data and Model Versioning

4. Automation

- **DevOps**: Automates the process of code integration, testing, and deployment through CI/CD pipelines. The focus is on managing the infrastructure and application delivery at scale.
- **MLOps**: Extends automation to include data preprocessing, model training, testing, and deployment, as well as model performance monitoring and retraining. MLOps introduces **continuous training (CT)** to ensure that models remain accurate over time as data evolves.

5. Continuous Delivery (CD) vs. Continuous Training (CT)

- **DevOps**: Focuses on **continuous delivery** (CD), which involves automating the testing and deployment of software to ensure rapid releases.
- **MLOps**: Introduces **continuous training (CT)** in addition to continuous delivery. This involves retraining models when new data arrives or when model performance degrades due to data drift or concept drift. MLOps also automates model deployment and monitoring to ensure they remain relevant.

6. Complexity of Models vs. Applications

- **DevOps**: The complexity revolves around managing code, application dependencies, and infrastructure. Standardization and automation of the CI/CD process are central to DevOps.
- **MLOps**: The complexity lies in managing **data**, **models**, and **code** together. Since models can degrade over time as data changes, MLOps has additional concerns like data versioning, model versioning, and drift detection, making the process more data-centric and dynamic than traditional software applications.

7. Monitoring and Maintenance

- **DevOps**: Monitoring is focused on the health of applications (e.g., uptime, errors, latency). Maintenance involves updating the application or fixing bugs when issues are detected.
- **MLOps**: Monitoring extends to **model performance** in addition to application health. It includes tracking metrics like model accuracy, precision, recall, and detecting model drift. MLOps requires mechanisms to automatically trigger model retraining when performance deteriorates.

8. Testing

- **DevOps**: Involves testing the software code for bugs, functionality, and performance. Unit tests, integration tests, and end-to-end tests are common.
- **MLOps**: Involves not only testing code but also testing models for accuracy, bias, and fairness. This requires validation on training and validation datasets to ensure the model generalizes well. Additionally, MLOps may include **A/B testing** to compare model versions in production.

9. Version Control

- **DevOps**: Uses version control for managing software code and configurations (e.g., Git for versioning code).
- **MLOps**: Uses version control not only for code but also for **datasets** and **models**. Tools like DVC (Data Version Control) or MLFlow help track experiments, model versions, and dataset changes to ensure reproducibility.

10. Handling Infrastructure

- **DevOps**: Manages the infrastructure required to deploy and run applications (e.g., servers, cloud instances, networking).
- **MLOps**: In addition to traditional infrastructure management, MLOps handles **specialized hardware** requirements like GPUs for model training, data pipelines for data ingestion, and cloud services for large-scale model deployment.

Conclusion

While DevOps and MLOps share foundational practices like CI/CD and automation, MLOps is specifically tailored to the unique challenges of managing machine learning models in production. DevOps focuses on software applications, while MLOps is concerned with the full lifecycle of machine learning, including data management, model development, and ongoing model monitoring and retraining. MLOps adds complexity due to the dynamic nature of data and models, making it a specialized extension of DevOps for AI-driven applications.

Benefits of MLOps for Scaling Machine Learning

MLOps (Machine Learning Operations) provides a structured framework that enables the effective deployment, monitoring, and management of machine learning models at scale. Here are the key benefits of MLOps for scaling machine learning:

1. Continuous Integration and Continuous Deployment (CI/CD)

MLOps integrates continuous integration (CI) and continuous deployment (CD) principles, allowing data scientists and developers to build, test, and deploy machine learning models in an automated, scalable manner. This ensures that models are updated frequently and deployed without human intervention, improving operational efficiency.

2. Automated Model Retraining and Monitoring

MLOps enables the automation of model retraining and monitoring pipelines. As new data is ingested, the system can automatically retrain models to keep them relevant, avoiding performance degradation due to data drift. This continuous training (CT) cycle ensures that models remain accurate over time.

3. Faster Time to Production

By automating the deployment and management of machine learning models, MLOps significantly reduces the time required to bring models into production. Automated workflows eliminate bottlenecks, allowing businesses to deploy models faster, which is critical for time-sensitive use cases like fraud detection or real-time personalization.

4. Scalability of Machine Learning Pipelines

MLOps helps scale machine learning pipelines by automating tasks such as data preprocessing, model training, hyperparameter tuning, and deployment. This scalability allows organizations to handle increasing amounts of data and deploy more models simultaneously without compromising efficiency.

5. Improved Collaboration Between Teams

MLOps fosters collaboration between data scientists, machine learning engineers, and IT/DevOps teams. By unifying the machine learning and software development lifecycle, teams can work together more effectively, ensuring that models are deployed and maintained in production environments efficiently and without delays.

6. Model Versioning and Reproducibility

MLOps tools facilitate version control for both models and datasets, ensuring that all changes are tracked and that experiments are reproducible. This versioning capability makes it easier to rollback to previous versions if a newly deployed model performs poorly, while also ensuring model compliance in regulated industries.

7. Enhanced Model Governance and Compliance

As machine learning is increasingly applied in regulated industries like finance and healthcare, MLOps provides tools for ensuring governance and compliance. With MLOps, organizations can track and audit model changes, datasets, and performance, ensuring that models meet industry standards and regulatory requirements.

8. Data and Model Pipeline Automation

MLOps automates the end-to-end machine learning lifecycle, from data collection and preprocessing to model training, evaluation, and deployment. Automated pipelines ensure that model development is repeatable, scalable, and adaptable to changes in the data.

9. Efficient Resource Management

MLOps enables the efficient allocation and utilization of resources such as compute power and storage. By leveraging cloud-based infrastructure or containerization technologies like Kubernetes and Docker, MLOps ensures that organizations can scale resources dynamically to meet the demands of training large models or handling high traffic in production.

10. Monitoring and Performance Metrics

With MLOps, models are continuously monitored after deployment. Organizations can track key performance metrics (e.g., accuracy, precision, recall) and detect anomalies or model degradation in real-time. This allows teams to address issues quickly, improving model reliability and performance in production environments.

11. Reduction of Technical Debt

MLOps practices reduce technical debt by establishing robust, automated workflows that ensure code, data, and models are well-maintained. This minimizes the accumulation of ad-hoc scripts and manual processes, making it easier to scale machine learning initiatives in a sustainable way.

12. Improved Model Security and Reliability

MLOps incorporates security best practices such as access control, audit logs, and encryption to protect sensitive data and models. Ensuring model integrity and security is crucial for applications in industries like finance, healthcare, and cybersecurity, where compromised models could have serious consequences.

13. Flexibility and Adaptability

As the machine learning landscape evolves, MLOps provides the flexibility to adopt new tools, frameworks, and algorithms. This adaptability ensures that organizations can stay at the forefront of innovation while scaling their machine learning operations.

Conclusion

MLOps delivers significant benefits for scaling machine learning by providing automation, collaboration, and governance across the entire machine learning lifecycle. With its ability to streamline workflows, enhance collaboration, and ensure the reliability of models in production, MLOps is a critical enabler for organizations aiming to scale their machine learning operations while ensuring agility and efficiency.

Chapter-2 Understanding the Machine Learning Lifecycle

Data Collection and Preparation with MLOps (using Python, Pandas& DVC)

In this example, we'll demonstrate how to automate **data collection**, **preparation**, and **versioning** using common MLOps tools and frameworks like **Pandas** for data manipulation and **DVC (Data Version Control)** for versioning and tracking datasets. This approach allows seamless integration of the data lifecycle into an MLOps pipeline.

1. Setting Up MLOps with DVC for Data Collection and Preparation

Prerequisites:

- Python installed

- Pandas installed (pip install pandas)
- DVC installed (pip install dvc)
- Git initialized in your project folder (git init)

Step 1: Data Collection

We will use Python and Pandas to collect data, simulate reading from a CSV file (could be fetched from a database or API in a real-world application), and then prepare it for machine learning.

```python
# data_collection.py

import pandas as pd


# Simulating data collection (read from a CSV file, API, or database)
def collect_data():
    # Simulate raw data collection from a source
    data = {
        'ID': [1, 2, 3, 4, 5],
        'Name': ['Alice', 'Bob', 'Charlie', 'David', 'Eve'],
        'Age': [25, 30, 35, 40, 22],
        'Salary': [50000, 60000, 70000, 80000, 55000]
    }

    df = pd.DataFrame(data)
    return df


# Save collected data as raw data
def save_raw_data(df, path='data/raw_data.csv'):
```

```
df.to_csv(path, index=False)

print(f"Raw data saved to {path}")


if __name__ == "__main__":

    df = collect_data()

    save_raw_data(df)
```

Run this script to simulate data collection:

```
python data_collection.py
```

This will generate a CSV file (data/raw_data.csv) that contains the raw data we'll work with.

Step 2: Data Preparation

After collecting the data, we need to clean and preprocess it before training machine learning models. This involves tasks like handling missing values, encoding categorical data, and normalizing numeric values.

```
# data_preparation.py

import pandas as pd

from sklearn.preprocessing import StandardScaler


# Simulating data preprocessing

def             preprocess_data(input_path='data/raw_data.csv',
output_path='data/prepared_data.csv'):

    # Load raw data

    df = pd.read_csv(input_path)


    # Drop rows with missing values (for simplicity)
```

```
df.dropna(inplace=True)


# Standardize the 'Age' and 'Salary' columns

scaler = StandardScaler()

df[['Age', 'Salary']] = scaler.fit_transform(df[['Age', 'Salary']])


# Save the preprocessed data

df.to_csv(output_path, index=False)

print(f"Preprocessed data saved to {output_path}")


if __name__ == "__main__":

    preprocess_data()
```

Run this script to preprocess the data:

```
python data_preparation.py
```

This will generate a CSV file (data/prepared_data.csv) that contains the preprocessed data ready for model training.

Step 3: Versioning Data with DVC

To keep track of your datasets (both raw and preprocessed), you can use **DVC (Data Version Control)** to manage versions of your data files, just like how Git tracks code versions.

1. **Initialize DVC in your project:**

   ```
   dvc init
   ```

2. **Add raw data to DVC:**

   ```
   dvc add data/raw_data.csv
   ```

This will track the raw data file using DVC and create a .dvc file (data/raw_data.csv.dvc), which you can commit to Git for versioning.

3. **Commit the changes:**

git add data/raw_data.csv.dvc .gitignore

git commit -m "Add raw data and DVC tracking"

4. **Add preprocessed data to DVC:**

   dvc add data/prepared_data.csv

5. **Commit preprocessed data versioning:**

   git add data/prepared_data.csv.dvc

   git commit -m "Add preprocessed data with DVC tracking"

Step 4: DVC Workflow for Data Versioning

Once your data is tracked with DVC, you can:

- **Push** the data to remote storage (like AWS S3, GCP, or local storage) by configuring DVC remotes.
- **Pull** the specific versions of data as needed to ensure reproducibility in the MLOps pipeline.

Example to configure a remote and push the data:

1. **Set up a DVC remote** (e.g., AWS S3, GCS, or a local directory):

dvc remote add -d myremote s3://mybucket/dvcstore

2. **Push your data to remote storage:**

   dvc push

3. **Pull your data version back when needed:**

dvc pull

Step 5: Automating Data Pipelines with DVC Pipelines

DVC allows you to create end-to-end pipelines that automatically handle data collection, preparation, and model training in one workflow.

Here's how to define the pipeline using DVC:

1. **Create a DVC pipeline stage for data collection:**

dvc   run   -n   collect_data   -d   data_collection.py   -o data/raw_data.csv python data_collection.py

2. **Create a DVC pipeline stage for data preparation:**

dvc   run   -n   preprocess_data   -d   data/raw_data.csv   -d data_preparation.py   -o   data/prepared_data.csv   python data_preparation.py

3. **Visualize the DVC pipeline:**

dvc dag

1. This will show the flow of your pipeline, ensuring reproducibility and traceability.

Summary of Key Benefits

- **Automated Data Collection**: Data collection processes are automated using Python and Pandas, ensuring data is consistently gathered from sources.
- **Data Preparation**: Data preprocessing tasks like scaling and cleaning are automated, creating clean and standardized datasets for model training.
- **Version Control with DVC**: Using DVC ensures that every dataset version (raw and preprocessed) is tracked, making the entire machine learning workflow reproducible and scalable.

- **Pipeline Automation**: With DVC pipelines, the data collection and preparation processes are fully automated, making it easy to rerun workflows when data or code changes.

This approach integrates **data collection**, **preparation**, and **versioning** into a robust MLOps pipeline, ensuring that data management is scalable and reproducible across teams and environments.

Model Development and Training using MLOps (with Python, Scikit-learn, and DVC)

In this example, we will explore how to integrate **model development**, **training**, and **versioning** within an **MLOps pipeline** using common tools like **Python**, **Scikit-learn**, and **DVC**. This ensures that the entire machine learning lifecycle, from data preparation to model deployment, is streamlined and reproducible.

Step 1: Setting Up Model Development and Training

We will begin by developing a simple machine learning model, using **Scikit-learn** for training, and versioning the code and model artifacts using **DVC**.

Install Required Libraries:

pip install scikit-learn pandas dvc

Step 2: Building and Training the Model

We will create a script to train a machine learning model. In this case, we'll use a **Logistic Regression** model to predict a binary outcome based on our preprocessed data.

```
# model_training.py

import pandas as pd

from sklearn.model_selection import train_test_split

from sklearn.linear_model import LogisticRegression

from sklearn.metrics import accuracy_score

import joblib


# Load the preprocessed data

def load_data(path='data/prepared_data.csv'):

    df = pd.read_csv(path)

    X = df[['Age', 'Salary']]  # Features

    y = df['ID']  # Target (for simplicity, using ID as a placeholder)

    return train_test_split(X, y, test_size=0.2, random_state=42)


# Train the model

def train_model(X_train, y_train):

    model = LogisticRegression()

    model.fit(X_train, y_train)

    return model


# Evaluate the model
```

```python
def evaluate_model(model, X_test, y_test):
    predictions = model.predict(X_test)
    accuracy = accuracy_score(y_test, predictions)
    print(f"Model Accuracy: {accuracy:.2f}")
    return accuracy


# Save the trained model
def save_model(model, path='models/logistic_regression_model.pkl'):
    joblib.dump(model, path)
    print(f"Model saved to {path}")


if __name__ == "__main__":
    # Load data
    X_train, X_test, y_train, y_test = load_data()

    # Train the model
    model = train_model(X_train, y_train)

    # Evaluate the model
    evaluate_model(model, X_test, y_test)

    # Save the model
    save_model(model)
```

This script will load the preprocessed data, train a logistic regression model, evaluate it, and save the model as a .pkl file.

Step 3: Versioning Model Artifacts with DVC

To ensure that both the **trained model** and the **training dataset** are versioned and reproducible, we will use **DVC** to track these artifacts.

1. **Initialize DVC if not already done:**

   dvc init

2. **Add the preprocessed data to DVC:**

   dvc add data/prepared_data.csv

3. **Add the trained model to DVC:**

After running the model training script, track the generated model file using DVC:

dvc add models/logistic_regression_model.pkl

4. **Create a DVC pipeline for model training:**

We will define a DVC pipeline to automate the entire process of loading data, training the model, and saving it. The pipeline will ensure that we can reproduce the training process anytime.

dvc run -n train_model \

  -d model_training.py \

  -d data/prepared_data.csv \

  -o models/logistic_regression_model.pkl \

  python model_training.py

☐   This command creates a DVC pipeline stage named train_model, which tracks the dependencies (data and script) and output (trained model). DVC generates a pipeline that automatically executes the training process.

5. **Commit your changes to Git:**

Once your model and data are versioned, commit everything to Git:

git add data/prepared_data.csv.dvc models/logistic_regression_model.pkl.dvc dvc.yaml dvc.lock

git commit -m "Add model training pipeline"

Step 4: Automating the MLOps Pipeline

The pipeline can now be executed automatically, ensuring that any changes in data or model code are reflected in the entire machine learning lifecycle.

1. **Modify and Retrain**: Whenever you modify the data or model, simply run the following command to trigger the pipeline:

   dvc repro

This will automatically retrain the model if any changes occur in the data or the training script.

2. **Pipeline Visualization**: You can visualize the entire pipeline using:

   dvc dag

1. This shows the workflow, illustrating how data flows through the model training process.

Step 5: Pushing Models and Data to Remote Storage

For collaboration or deployment, you might want to store datasets and models in remote storage (e.g., AWS S3, Google

Cloud Storage). DVC allows you to **push** and **pull** data to and from these remote locations.

1. **Set up a remote storage (e.g., S3):**

   dvc remote add -d myremote s3://mybucket/dvcstore

2. **Push your data and model to remote storage:**

   dvc push

3. **Pull the exact data or model versions later:**

   dvc pull

This ensures that all collaborators or deployment environments can access the exact version of the data and models used during development.

Step 6: Model Evaluation and Logging

In MLOps, it is critical to monitor and log model performance over time. We can integrate evaluation metrics logging with tools like **MLflow**, or simply log results to a file in this basic example.

```
# model_evaluation.py

def log_metrics(accuracy, path='logs/metrics.txt'):

    with open(path, 'a') as f:

        f.write(f"Model Accuracy: {accuracy:.2f}\n")

    print(f"Metrics logged to {path}")
```

After evaluating the model, we can log the metrics to a text file or integrate with a more comprehensive tracking solution like MLflow for advanced logging and monitoring.

Step 7: Deploying the Trained Model

Once the model is trained and logged, you can package it for deployment in various environments, whether in **Docker**, **Kubernetes**, or as a web service using **Flask** or **FastAPI**.

A simple deployment script using **Flask** can look like this:

```python
# flask_deployment.py
from flask import Flask, request, jsonify
import joblib


app = Flask(__name__)


# Load the model
model = joblib.load('models/logistic_regression_model.pkl')


@app.route('/predict', methods=['POST'])
def predict():
    data = request.get_json()
    age = data['age']
    salary = data['salary']
    prediction = model.predict([[age, salary]])[0]
    return jsonify({'prediction': int(prediction)})


if __name__ == '__main__':
    app.run(debug=True)
```

This will serve the model as a REST API endpoint, allowing external systems to send data and receive predictions.

Summary of Key Benefits

- **Automated Model Training**: Training and evaluation of models are automated with DVC pipelines, ensuring reproducibility.
- **Versioning Models**: Every model artifact, along with the data used to train it, is versioned, making it easy to track and roll back to previous models.
- **Seamless Collaboration**: Using DVC's remote storage capabilities, data scientists can collaborate across teams while maintaining data and model integrity.
- **Deployability**: The trained models can be deployed using frameworks like Flask, ensuring that machine learning services can be rapidly integrated into production environments.

With this setup, you can efficiently manage the entire **machine learning lifecycle** using **MLOps principles**, from data preparation and model development to deployment and version control.

Model Validation and Testing in MLOps

Model validation and **testing** are crucial phases in the machine learning lifecycle, ensuring that the model is generalizable, performs well on unseen data, and is free of overfitting. In **MLOps (Machine Learning Operations)**, the goal is to automate these processes, making them reproducible, scalable, and efficient.

This detailed explanation covers how to set up **model validation** and **testing** within an MLOps pipeline using **Python**, **Scikit-learn**, **DVC**, and **MLflow**.

Step 1: Understanding Model Validation

In machine learning, **model validation** is the process of evaluating the model's performance on a holdout dataset that was not used during training. This ensures that the model can generalize to unseen data. Common validation strategies include:

1. **Train-Test Split**: Dividing the dataset into training and testing subsets.
2. **Cross-Validation**: Splitting the dataset into k folds and validating the model on each fold.
3. **Stratified Sampling**: Ensuring balanced distribution of classes when performing cross-validation on classification tasks.

Step 2: Model Validation Workflow in MLOps

In an MLOps pipeline, the **validation** and **testing** processes should be automated. This involves:

- **Tracking performance metrics** after every model training run.
- **Versioning models** and their performance data for traceability.
- **Comparing different models** to select the best one for production.

Here, we'll use **Scikit-learn** for the model and **DVC** for version control, as well as **MLflow** for logging model performance metrics.

Step 3: Code for Model Validation with Cross-Validation

We will validate a model using **cross-validation** and log the results. Let's modify the previous logistic regression example to include **cross-validation**.

```
# model_validation.py

import pandas as pd
```

```python
from sklearn.model_selection import train_test_split,
cross_val_score

from sklearn.linear_model import LogisticRegression

from sklearn.metrics import accuracy_score

import joblib

import mlflow


# Load the data
def load_data(path='data/prepared_data.csv'):
    df = pd.read_csv(path)
    X = df[['Age', 'Salary']]  # Features
    y = df['Target']  # Target label
    return train_test_split(X, y, test_size=0.2, random_state=42)


# Train the model using cross-validation
def train_and_validate_model(X, y, model=LogisticRegression(),
cv=5):
    scores = cross_val_score(model, X, y, cv=cv)
    print(f"Cross-validation accuracy scores: {scores}")
    print(f"Mean accuracy: {scores.mean():.2f}")
    return model.fit(X, y), scores


# Save the model
def                                    save_model(model,
path='models/logistic_regression_model.pkl'):
    joblib.dump(model, path)
```

```
print(f"Model saved to {path}")

if __name__ == "__main__":
    # Load the data
    X_train, X_test, y_train, y_test = load_data()

    # Log metrics to MLflow
    with mlflow.start_run():
        # Train the model with cross-validation
        model, cv_scores = train_and_validate_model(X_train, y_train)

        # Log cross-validation accuracy to MLflow
        mlflow.log_metric("cross_val_accuracy", cv_scores.mean())

        # Save the model
        save_model(model)
```

Explanation:

- **Cross-Validation**: The cross_val_score function from Scikit-learn is used to perform 5-fold cross-validation. The function splits the data into five subsets, trains the model on four of them, and evaluates it on the fifth.
- **MLflow Logging**: The mlflow.log_metric() function logs the cross-validation accuracy to MLflow, so the model's performance can be tracked over time. You can compare these metrics across different models and runs.

Step 4: Model Testing and Evaluation on Holdout Test Set

Once the model is validated, it's critical to test it on a holdout test set to ensure it performs well on completely unseen data.

Here's how we can extend our script to include **testing**:

```python
# model_testing.py
from sklearn.metrics import accuracy_score, classification_report


# Evaluate the model on the holdout test set
def test_model(model, X_test, y_test):
    predictions = model.predict(X_test)
    accuracy = accuracy_score(y_test, predictions)
    report = classification_report(y_test, predictions)
    print(f"Test Accuracy: {accuracy:.2f}")
    print(f"Classification Report:\n{report}")
    return accuracy, report


if __name__ == "__main__":
    # Load the data
    X_train, X_test, y_train, y_test = load_data()

    # Train and validate the model
    model, _ = train_and_validate_model(X_train, y_train)

    # Test the model on the holdout set
```

test_accuracy, classification_report = test_model(model, X_test, y_test)

Log test accuracy to MLflow

with mlflow.start_run():

mlflow.log_metric("test_accuracy", test_accuracy)

Explanation:

- **Test Model**: We use the accuracy_score and classification_report from Scikit-learn to evaluate the model on the holdout test set.
- **MLflow Logging**: The test accuracy is logged to MLflow for easy comparison and monitoring.

Step 5: Automating the Validation and Testing Workflow with DVC

In MLOps, automation is key. We can automate the entire **model training**, **validation**, and **testing pipeline** using **DVC**.

1. **Create a DVC stage for testing:**

   To automate the testing process, we can add another DVC stage to the pipeline for model testing:

   dvc run -n test_model \

   -d model_testing.py \

   -d models/logistic_regression_model.pkl \

   -o logs/test_results.txt \

   python model_testing.py

This command creates a DVC stage that tracks the dependencies (model_testing.py, the trained model) and outputs (test_results.txt, where the test results will be saved).

2. **Run the entire pipeline:**

After setting up the DVC pipeline, you can run the entire workflow from data preparation to model validation and testing by simply running:

dvc repro

1. This command ensures that the pipeline automatically runs all steps, including data loading, model training, validation, and testing.

Step 6: Monitoring Model Performance and Drift

Once the model is deployed in production, it's essential to monitor its performance and detect **model drift** (when the model's accuracy deteriorates over time due to changes in the data).

Here are steps to monitor model drift:

1. **Track Model Performance Over Time**: Use a logging tool like **MLflow** or **Prometheus** to track metrics such as accuracy and precision continuously. Compare current performance against historical performance.
2. **Set Alerts for Performance Drop**: In an MLOps setup, you can set up alerts to notify the team if the model's performance drops below a threshold.
3. **Re-trigger Retraining**: If model drift is detected, the pipeline can be automatically triggered to retrain the model using new data. This can be achieved by adding hooks in your pipeline that monitor live data.

Step 7: Summary of MLOps Benefits for Validation and Testing

- **Automation**: DVC and MLflow allow you to fully automate the model validation and testing process, reducing manual overhead and ensuring reproducibility.
- **Versioning**: All models and data versions are tracked, making it easy to trace back the exact model used for validation or deployment.
- **Continuous Monitoring**: With tools like MLflow, you can continuously monitor the performance of models in production and detect issues like model drift early.
- **Reproducibility**: The pipeline ensures that the entire lifecycle—from training to testing—is reproducible across different environments and teams.

By integrating model validation, testing, and monitoring in an MLOps framework, machine learning models can be reliably developed, validated, and deployed at scale, with full automation and traceability.

Model Deployment and Monitoring in MLOps

Model Deployment and **Monitoring** are critical steps in the MLOps lifecycle, allowing machine learning models to be used in production environments and ensuring their ongoing performance over time. This guide covers the best practices and methodologies for deploying and monitoring machine learning models effectively.

Step 1: What is Model Deployment?

Model Deployment refers to the process of integrating a machine learning model into a production environment where it can make predictions based on new data. Successful deployment makes the model accessible to end users, applications, or services.

Common Deployment Strategies:

1. **Batch Inference**: Models are used to process large volumes of data at once (e.g., nightly jobs).
2. **Real-time Inference**: Models provide immediate predictions in response to user requests or events (e.g., web applications, APIs).
3. **Embedded Deployment**: Models are deployed in devices (e.g., mobile phones, IoT devices).

Step 2: Preparing for Deployment

Before deploying a model, ensure that the following steps are completed:

1. **Model Serialization**: Convert the trained model into a format suitable for deployment (e.g., using **joblib** or **pickle**).
2. **Containerization**: Use **Docker** to create a container that includes the model and its dependencies. This helps ensure consistency across environments.
3. **API Development**: Create an API (using **Flask** or **FastAPI**) to expose the model's functionality.

Step 3: Example Code for Model Deployment with Flask

Here's an example of deploying a machine learning model using **Flask**.

1. Save the Model

First, ensure that your trained model is saved:

Save the trained model

import joblib

```
model = ...  # Your trained model
joblib.dump(model, 'model.pkl')
```

2. Create a Flask API

Now, create a simple Flask application to serve predictions:

```python
# app.py
from flask import Flask, request, jsonify
import joblib
import numpy as np


app = Flask(__name__)


# Load the model
model = joblib.load('model.pkl')


@app.route('/predict', methods=['POST'])
def predict():
    data = request.get_json(force=True)
    features = np.array(data['features']).reshape(1, -1)
    prediction = model.predict(features)
    return jsonify({'prediction': prediction.tolist()})


if __name__ == '__main__':
    app.run(debug=True)
```

3. Run the Flask App

Run your Flask application:

python app.py

You can now send a POST request to the /predict endpoint with the required features in JSON format.

Step 4: Monitoring Model Performance

After deployment, it is crucial to continuously monitor the model to ensure it maintains performance. Key aspects of monitoring include:

1. **Performance Metrics**: Track accuracy, precision, recall, F1-score, etc. Use monitoring tools like **Prometheus** and **Grafana** to visualize metrics.
2. **Model Drift Detection**: Monitor incoming data and model predictions to detect shifts in data distribution (concept drift) or changes in the model's prediction quality (performance drift).
3. **Logging and Alerts**: Set up logging of model predictions, errors, and metrics. Configure alerts for when the model performance drops below a predefined threshold.

Example of Monitoring with Prometheus and Grafana

You can integrate **Prometheus** for metrics collection and **Grafana** for visualization.

1. **Install Prometheus and Grafana**.
2. Use a Python library like **prometheus_client** to expose metrics in your Flask app.

from prometheus_client import PrometheusMetrics

metrics = PrometheusMetrics(app)

```
@app.route('/metrics', methods=['GET'])

def metrics_route():

    return metrics.metrics()
```

3. Configure Prometheus to scrape metrics from your Flask application.
4. Set up dashboards in Grafana to visualize the metrics over time.

Step 5: Model Retraining

Over time, models can become less accurate due to changing data patterns. To address this:

1. **Automate Retraining**: Use tools like **DVC** to trigger retraining based on new data or performance metrics.
2. **Version Control**: Keep track of model versions and datasets to ensure reproducibility.
3. **Continuous Integration/Continuous Deployment (CI/CD)**: Implement CI/CD pipelines for seamless updates to the model.

Step 6: Summary of Deployment and Monitoring in MLOps

- **Deployment**: Ensure your model is accessible and usable through APIs. Use containerization for consistency.
- **Monitoring**: Continuously track model performance and data drift. Use logging and alerting to stay informed about model health.
- **Automated Retraining**: Set up pipelines to retrain the model as necessary to maintain performance.

By following these best practices, you can effectively deploy and monitor machine learning models, ensuring they deliver reliable results in production environments. This approach enhances the overall robustness of your machine learning operations and helps maintain a high level of accuracy and performance over time.

Chapter-3 Core Components of MLOps

Continuous Integration (CI) in Machine Learning using MLOps

Continuous Integration (CI) in Machine Learning (ML) refers to the practice of automatically testing and integrating changes to the codebase, models, and data into a shared repository. It ensures that new changes do not break existing functionality and helps maintain the overall health of the ML system. This is especially important in MLOps, where model development involves not just code, but also data and configuration.

This guide will walk you through setting up CI for an ML project using tools like GitHub Actions, pytest, and Docker.

Step 1: Setting Up Your Project Structure

Ensure your project has a clear structure. Here's a simple example:

my_ml_project/

|

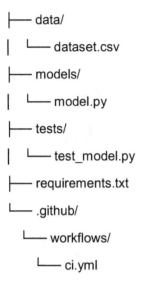

```
├── data/
│   └── dataset.csv
├── models/
│   └── model.py
├── tests/
│   └── test_model.py
├── requirements.txt
└── .github/
    └── workflows/
        └── ci.yml
```

Step 2: Writing Your Model Code

Create a simple model in models/model.py. For demonstration, we'll create a simple function that trains a linear regression model:

```python
# models/model.py

import pandas as pd

from sklearn.linear_model import LinearRegression

from sklearn.model_selection import train_test_split

import joblib


def train_model(data_path):
    # Load dataset
    data = pd.read_csv(data_path)
    X = data[['feature1', 'feature2']]
    y = data['target']
```

```python
# Split data
X_train, X_test, y_train, y_test = train_test_split(X, y, test_size=0.2, random_state=42)

# Train model
model = LinearRegression()
model.fit(X_train, y_train)

# Save model
joblib.dump(model, 'models/model.pkl')
return model
```

Step 3: Writing Tests

Create a test for your model in tests/test_model.py:

```python
# tests/test_model.py
import pytest
from models.model import train_model
import os

def test_train_model():
    # Path to the dataset
    data_path = os.path.join('data', 'dataset.csv')

    # Ensure the model can be trained
```

```
model = train_model(data_path)


    # Check if model was saved

    assert os.path.exists('models/model.pkl')
```

Step 4: Creating a Requirements File

Create a requirements.txt file with your dependencies:

pandas

scikit-learn

joblib

pytest

Step 5: Setting Up CI with GitHub Actions

Create a CI workflow configuration file in .github/workflows/ci.yml:

```
# .github/workflows/ci.yml
name: CI


on:
  push:
    branches: [ main ]
  pull_request:
    branches: [ main ]


jobs:
```

```
build:
  runs-on: ubuntu-latest

  steps:
  - name: Checkout code
    uses: actions/checkout@v2

  - name: Set up Python
    uses: actions/setup-python@v2
    with:
      python-version: '3.8'

  - name: Install dependencies
    run: |
      python -m pip install --upgrade pip
      pip install -r requirements.txt

  - name: Run tests
    run: |
      pytest tests/
```

Step 6: Running CI Pipeline

1. **Push Changes**: Commit your changes to the repository and push them to GitHub.
2. **Check Actions Tab**: Navigate to the "Actions" tab in your GitHub repository to view the CI pipeline running. It

will execute the steps defined in your CI configuration file.

3. **Review Results**: If all tests pass, your CI setup is successful! If any tests fail, you can troubleshoot based on the logs provided by GitHub Actions.

Conclusion

By setting up Continuous Integration for your machine learning project using MLOps practices, you ensure that your code, models, and data changes are consistently tested and integrated. This approach helps maintain the quality and reliability of your machine learning systems and supports collaboration within your team.

In summary, you have:

- Set up a project structure.
- Created a simple model.
- Written tests for your model.
- Configured CI using GitHub Actions to automate the testing and integration process.

This workflow can be further expanded to include additional steps like model validation, deployment, and monitoring, making it a comprehensive MLOps pipeline.

Continuous Deployment (CD) for Machine Learning Models using MLOps

Continuous Deployment (CD) is an essential aspect of MLOps that automates the deployment of machine learning models into production. This process ensures that new models or updates to existing models can be released frequently and reliably, thereby improving the overall efficiency of the machine learning lifecycle.

This guide will walk you through the key concepts of Continuous Deployment for ML models, best practices, and a practical implementation example.

Key Concepts of Continuous Deployment in MLOps

1. **Model Registry**:
   - A centralized repository that stores model artifacts and metadata. It keeps track of various model versions, making it easier to manage deployments and rollbacks.
2. **Automated Testing**:
   - Before deployment, models should be subjected to various tests, including unit tests, integration tests, and performance tests, to ensure they meet quality standards.
3. **Deployment Strategies**:
   - Different strategies can be employed for deploying models, including:
     - **Blue-Green Deployment**: Two identical environments are maintained; one is live, and the other is idle. New versions are deployed to the idle environment, and traffic is switched once the new version is validated.
     - **Canary Releases**: A small percentage of users receive the new version initially. Based on feedback and performance, the deployment can be scaled to all users.
     - **Shadow Deployment**: The new model runs in parallel with the old one, receiving live traffic but not impacting users. Performance metrics are monitored before a full rollout.
4. **Monitoring and Feedback Loop**:
   - After deployment, models should be continuously monitored for performance, accuracy, and any drifts in the data. A feedback loop helps in iterating and improving models.
5. **Rollback Mechanism**:

    o   In case a deployment causes issues, having a rollback mechanism allows reverting to a stable version quickly.

Steps for Implementing Continuous Deployment for ML Models

Step 1: Setup Your Project Structure

A typical project structure may look like this:

```
ml_project/
|
├── models/
|   ├── model.py
|   └── model_registry.py
├── tests/
|   └── test_model.py
├── deployment/
|   └── deploy_model.py
├── requirements.txt
└── .github/
    └── workflows/
        └── cd.yml
```

Step 2: Create a Model Registry

The model registry will track model versions and metadata. A simple implementation might look like this:

```
# models/model_registry.py
class ModelRegistry:
```

```python
def __init__(self):
    self.models = {}


def register_model(self, model_name, version, model_path):
    self.models[model_name] = {'version': version, 'path': model_path}


def get_model(self, model_name):
    return self.models.get(model_name)
```

Step 3: Write Deployment Scripts

Create a deployment script in deployment/deploy_model.py that loads the model and deploys it:

```python
# deployment/deploy_model.py
import joblib
from models.model_registry import ModelRegistry


def deploy_model(model_name):
    registry = ModelRegistry()
    model_info = registry.get_model(model_name)

    if model_info:
        model = joblib.load(model_info['path'])
        # Here you would add code to deploy the model to a service (like AWS, GCP, etc.)
        print(f"Deploying {model_name} version {model_info['version']}")
```

```
else:

    print("Model not found in registry.")
```

Step 4: Setup Automated Testing

Write tests to ensure that the model behaves as expected. Place your tests in tests/test_model.py:

```
# tests/test_model.py

import pytest

from models.model import train_model


def test_model_training():

    model = train_model('data/dataset.csv')

    assert model is not None  # Ensure the model was trained
```

Step 5: CI/CD Configuration

Set up a Continuous Deployment workflow using GitHub Actions in .github/workflows/cd.yml:

```
# .github/workflows/cd.yml

name: Continuous Deployment


on:
  push:
    branches: [ main ]


jobs:
  deploy:
```

```
runs-on: ubuntu-latest

steps:
- name: Checkout code
  uses: actions/checkout@v2

- name: Set up Python
  uses: actions/setup-python@v2
  with:
    python-version: '3.8'

- name: Install dependencies
  run: |
    python -m pip install --upgrade pip
    pip install -r requirements.txt

- name: Run tests
  run: |
    pytest tests/

- name: Deploy Model
  run: |
    python deployment/deploy_model.py
```

Step 6: Monitoring and Feedback

Once the model is deployed, implement monitoring for model performance and user feedback. You can use logging frameworks to collect metrics and visualize performance over time.

Best Practices for Continuous Deployment

1. **Automate Everything**: Automate the deployment, testing, and monitoring processes to reduce manual errors and increase efficiency.
2. **Use Version Control**: Keep all your code, configurations, and models version-controlled for better traceability.
3. **Ensure Data Quality**: Regularly monitor data inputs for changes that could affect model performance (data drift).
4. **Implement Rollbacks**: Always have a rollback strategy to revert to a previous stable version if necessary.
5. **Engage with Stakeholders**: Collect feedback from users and stakeholders to continuously improve the model and its deployment.

Conclusion

Continuous Deployment in MLOps is a critical component for automating the release of machine learning models into production. By implementing CD, organizations can enhance their ability to deliver reliable models rapidly and efficiently. Following the steps outlined in this guide, including setting up a model registry, automated testing, and deployment workflows, will significantly streamline the process of managing ML models in production environments. By adhering to best practices, teams can ensure robust deployment pipelines that respond effectively to changing business needs and user feedback.

Automated Testing and Validation using MLOps

Automated testing and validation are crucial components of the MLOps (Machine Learning Operations) lifecycle, ensuring that machine learning models are robust, accurate, and ready for deployment in production environments. This process integrates software engineering best practices with machine learning workflows, facilitating the creation of reliable models while minimizing manual intervention. Here's a detailed overview of automated testing and validation in MLOps.

Key Components of Automated Testing and Validation

1. **Unit Testing**:
    o **Purpose**: Unit tests validate individual components of the codebase, such as data processing functions, feature engineering, and model training functions.
    o **Tools**: Common testing frameworks include **pytest** and **unittest** in Python.
    o **Example**: Testing a function that preprocesses data to ensure it returns the expected format and values.

```
# tests/test_data_processing.py

import pytest

from data_processing import preprocess_data


def test_preprocess_data():
    input_data = [1, 2, 3]
    expected_output = [0.0, 0.5, 1.0]   # Example expected output
```

```
    assert        preprocess_data(input_data)        ==
    expected_output
```

2. **Integration Testing**:

- **Purpose**: Integration tests check how different parts of the machine learning pipeline work together. This includes the interaction between data ingestion, preprocessing, model training, and prediction.
- **Example**: Verifying that the end-to-end pipeline can process data from start to finish without errors.

```python
# tests/test_integration.py

def test_end_to_end_pipeline():

    data = load_data('data/source.csv')

    preprocessed_data = preprocess_data(data)

    model = train_model(preprocessed_data)

    predictions = model.predict(preprocessed_data)

    assert len(predictions) == len(preprocessed_data)
```

3. **Model Validation**:

- **Purpose**: Model validation ensures that the trained model meets specified performance criteria before deployment. This can involve checking metrics such as accuracy, precision, recall, and F1-score against validation datasets.
- **Techniques**: Cross-validation, hold-out validation, and A/B testing are common techniques used to validate models.

```python
# validation/validate_model.py

from sklearn.metrics import accuracy_score


def validate_model(model, X_val, y_val):
```

```
predictions = model.predict(X_val)
```

```
accuracy = accuracy_score(y_val, predictions)
```

```
assert accuracy > 0.80, "Model accuracy is below threshold."
```

4. **Performance Testing**:

- **Purpose**: Performance tests evaluate how well the model performs under various conditions, including latency, throughput, and resource utilization. This is especially important for models that will be deployed in real-time applications.
- **Tools**: Load testing tools like **JMeter** or **Locust** can be utilized to simulate user requests and analyze performance metrics.

5. **Data Validation**:

- **Purpose**: Data validation checks ensure the quality and integrity of the data being used to train and evaluate models. It involves verifying data types, checking for missing values, and ensuring that data follows expected distributions.
- **Example**: Using libraries like **Great Expectations** for data validation.

```
# validation/validate_data.py
```

```
from great_expectations import DataContext
```

```
def validate_data(data):
    context = DataContext('path/to/great_expectations/directory')
    batch = context.get_batch('my_dataset')
```

```
results                                    =
context.run_validation_operator('action_list_operator',
assets_to_validate=[batch])

assert results['success'], "Data validation failed."
```

Implementation of Automated Testing and Validation in MLOps

1. **Set Up a Testing Framework**:
    o   Establish a testing framework that integrates with your CI/CD pipeline. This ensures that tests are executed automatically on code commits or pull requests.
2. **Create a Test Suite**:
    o   Develop a comprehensive suite of tests covering unit tests, integration tests, model validation, and performance tests. Ensure tests are organized and easily maintainable.
3. **Continuous Integration**:
    o   Utilize CI tools like **Jenkins**, **Travis CI**, or **GitHub Actions** to automate the testing process. These tools can run tests on every code change, providing immediate feedback on code quality.
4. **Monitoring Model Performance**:
    o   Once the model is deployed, set up monitoring tools to continuously assess model performance. Tools like **Prometheus** or **Grafana** can be used to visualize metrics and detect issues in real-time.
5. **Feedback Loop**:
    o   Incorporate a feedback mechanism where performance data can inform future model training and adjustments. This helps in refining models based on real-world performance.

Best Practices for Automated Testing and Validation in MLOps

1. **Automate Everything**: Aim for a fully automated testing process to reduce manual intervention and errors.

2. **Keep Tests Isolated**: Ensure unit tests are independent of each other to avoid cascading failures.
3. **Use Version Control**: Keep track of changes in both code and models. This makes it easier to identify issues when tests fail.
4. **Regularly Review Tests**: Periodically review and update tests to ensure they remain relevant as the codebase evolves.
5. **Implement Comprehensive Coverage**: Strive for high test coverage, ensuring that critical parts of the codebase are thoroughly tested.

Conclusion

Automated testing and validation in MLOps are essential for maintaining the quality, reliability, and performance of machine learning models throughout their lifecycle. By integrating these practices into the MLOps workflow, teams can confidently deploy models into production, knowing they have been rigorously tested and validated. Following best practices and leveraging appropriate tools will lead to smoother deployments, enhanced collaboration, and ultimately better-performing machine learning systems.

Chapter-4 Setting Up an MLOps Pipeline

Overview of the MLOps Pipeline

The MLOps (Machine Learning Operations) pipeline integrates machine learning with DevOps practices to streamline the development, deployment, and monitoring of ML models in production. It ensures that models are reproducible, scalable, and continuously improved. Here's a breakdown of the MLOps pipeline and a simple code example for each stage.

1. Data Ingestion and Preparation

This step involves collecting, cleaning, and preprocessing data for model training. Data is often split into training, validation, and testing sets.

```
import pandas as pd

from sklearn.model_selection import train_test_split


# Load and inspect dataset

data = pd.read_csv('dataset.csv')

print(data.head())
```

Split data into train and test sets

```
train_data, test_data = train_test_split(data, test_size=0.2,
random_state=42)
```

Data preprocessing (scaling, encoding, etc.)

```
from sklearn.preprocessing import StandardScaler

scaler = StandardScaler()

train_data_scaled = scaler.fit_transform(train_data)

test_data_scaled = scaler.transform(test_data)
```

2. **Model Development and Training**

In this phase, machine learning models are developed using training data. Multiple models might be tested for performance, such as linear regression, decision trees, or deep learning models.

```
from sklearn.linear_model import LinearRegression

from sklearn.metrics import mean_squared_error
```

Model training

```
model = LinearRegression()

model.fit(train_data_scaled[:, :-1], train_data_scaled[:, -1])
```

```
# Evaluate model

predictions = model.predict(test_data_scaled[:, :-1])

mse = mean_squared_error(test_data_scaled[:, -1], predictions)

print(f"Mean Squared Error: {mse}")
```

3. Model Validation

In this step, the model's performance is validated on unseen data (validation set) to ensure that it generalizes well.

```
from sklearn.model_selection import cross_val_score



# Perform cross-validation

cv_scores = cross_val_score(model, train_data_scaled[:, :-1], train_data_scaled[:, -1], cv=5)

print(f"Cross-validation scores: {cv_scores}")

print(f"Mean CV Score: {cv_scores.mean()}")
```

4. Model Deployment

The trained and validated model is deployed into a production environment. Docker is commonly used for containerization, and services like Kubernetes are employed for scalability.

```
# Create a Dockerfile for model deployment

FROM python:3.8-slim



WORKDIR /app
```

```
COPY . /app

RUN pip install -r requirements.txt


# Expose the necessary port

EXPOSE 5000


# Command to run the app

CMD ["python", "app.py"]
```

5. Continuous Integration (CI) and Continuous Deployment (CD)

CI/CD pipelines ensure that model updates are automatically tested, validated, and deployed with minimal manual intervention. Tools like Jenkins or GitLab CI can be used.

```
# Example GitLab CI pipeline

stages:

  - test

  - deploy


test:

  stage: test

  script:
```

```
  - pytest tests/
```

```
deploy:

  stage: deploy

  script:

    - docker build -t mlops_model .

    - docker push registry.example.com/mlops_model

    - kubectl apply -f deployment.yaml
```

6. **Model Monitoring and Retraining**

Once deployed, the model is monitored to ensure it performs well in production. Retraining might be required if model drift is detected (i.e., the model performance degrades over time due to changes in data).

```
import mlflow
```

```
# Log model performance metrics

mlflow.log_metric("mse", mse)

mlflow.log_param("model_type", "LinearRegression")
```

```
# Retrain model if drift is detected (example code)

if mse> threshold:
```

\# Retrain logic here

model.fit(train_data_scaled[:, :-1], train_data_scaled[:, -1])

mlflow.log_metric("retrained_mse", new_mse)

Conclusion

The MLOps pipeline combines traditional software engineering and machine learning best practices, enabling continuous integration, testing, and deployment of machine learning models in production.

Tools for MLOps: KubernetesVersion Control for Code and Data, Docker, and Jenkins

MLOps (Machine Learning Operations) involves a set of practices and tools that combine DevOps with machine learning to automate and optimize the deployment, monitoring, and management of machine learning models. Here's an overview of key tools used in MLOps for managing code, data, infrastructure, and continuous integration and deployment (CI/CD).

1. Kubernetes: Container Orchestration for Machine Learning Workflows

Kubernetes is a powerful container orchestration platform that automates the deployment, scaling, and management of containerized applications, making it a go-to choice for managing ML models in production environments.

- **Why Kubernetes for MLOps?**

- o **Scalability**: Automatically scales machine learning workloads based on demand.
- o **Reliability**: Ensures high availability and resilience of your services through self-healing features like restarting failed containers.
- o **Infrastructure Abstraction**: Kubernetes abstracts away underlying infrastructure, making it easy to deploy machine learning models across different environments (cloud, on-premise).
- **Kubernetes MLOps Example (Model Deployment)**

```
# Kubernetes YAML file for deploying a model

apiVersion: apps/v1

kind: Deployment

metadata:

  name: ml-model

spec:

  replicas: 2

  selector:

matchLabels:

    app: ml-model

  template:

    metadata:

    labels:

      app: ml-model
```

```
spec:

  containers:

  - name: ml-container

    image: registry.example.com/mlops_model:latest

    ports:

    - containerPort: 5000

---

apiVersion: v1

kind: Service

metadata:

  name: ml-model-service

spec:

  type: LoadBalancer

  ports:

  - port: 80

targetPort: 5000

  selector:

    app: ml-model
```

2. Version Control for Code and Data

Version control is essential in MLOps to track changes in both code and datasets. While Git is widely used for code, specialized tools like DVC (Data Version Control) and MLflow are used for tracking data and model versions.

- **Git for Code Versioning**
  - ○ Git is essential for version control of machine learning code, ensuring that every experiment, script, and configuration is reproducible and traceable.
- **DVC for Data and Model Versioning**
  - ○ DVC (Data Version Control) is used to track large datasets and ML models, providing version control over files that cannot be handled efficiently by Git.
- **Example: Versioning Data with DVC**

Initialize DVC in the project

dvcinit

Add large dataset to DVC

dvc add data/dataset.csv

Commit changes to Git

git add data/dataset.csv.dvc .gitignore

git commit -m "Add dataset for training"

3. Docker: Containerization for Reproducibility

Docker allows packaging machine learning applications with all dependencies, ensuring consistency between development, testing, and production environments. Docker containers encapsulate everything (code, libraries, and environment) needed to run the model, providing a portable and reproducible solution.

- **Benefits of Docker in MLOps:**
  - ○ **Reproducibility**: Ensures that the model runs the same in different environments.
  - ○ **Isolation**: Containers isolate the ML application and its dependencies, preventing conflicts with other services.
  - ○ **Portability**: Docker images can be deployed on any platform that supports containers, making deployment easier and faster.
- **Dockerfile Example for Model Deployment**

```
# Base image

FROM python:3.8-slim



# Set working directory

WORKDIR /app



# Copy the model code and install dependencies

COPY . /app

RUN pip install -r requirements.txt



# Expose the port

EXPOSE 5000
```

```
# Command to run the model
```

```
CMD ["python", "app.py"]
```

4. Jenkins: Continuous Integration/Continuous Deployment (CI/CD)

Jenkins is a popular open-source automation server that facilitates CI/CD pipelines. In MLOps, Jenkins automates the entire ML pipeline, including testing, building, and deploying models into production. It integrates with other MLOps tools like Docker and Kubernetes to ensure continuous delivery of ML models.

- **Why Jenkins for MLOps?**
    - **Automated Testing**: Automatically tests the model code at each stage of development.
    - **Continuous Deployment**: Deploy models into production as soon as they are validated.
    - **Integration**: Jenkins integrates seamlessly with Git, Docker, and Kubernetes, making it ideal for MLOps pipelines.
- **Jenkins CI/CD Pipeline for Machine Learning**

```
pipeline {

    agent any

    stages {

stage('Clone Repository') {

        steps {

            git 'https://github.com/your-repo/ml-project.git'

        }

    }
```

```
stage('Build Docker Image') {

        steps {

            script {

dockerImage = docker.build("mlops_model:${env.BUILD_ID}")

                }

            }

        }

stage('Run Tests') {

        steps {

sh 'pytest tests/'

                }

            }

stage('Deploy to Kubernetes') {

        steps {

sh 'kubectl apply -f k8s-deployment.yaml'

                }

            }

        }

}
```

Conclusion

By leveraging **Kubernetes** for orchestration, **Docker** for containerization, **Git/DVC** for version control, and **Jenkins** for CI/CD, MLOps enables the seamless integration of machine learning models into production environments. These tools together ensure a scalable, automated, and reliable machine learning lifecycle—from development to deployment and monitoring.

CI/CD Pipelines for Machine Learning Projects

Continuous Integration and Continuous Deployment (CI/CD) pipelines in machine learning (ML) projects are crucial for automating and streamlining the development, testing, deployment, and monitoring of ML models. By implementing CI/CD pipelines, organizations can ensure faster, reliable, and scalable deployment of machine learning models into production environments.

1. What is CI/CD in Machine Learning?

- **Continuous Integration (CI)**: Automates the integration of code changes (features, fixes) from multiple contributors into a shared repository. Each change is automatically tested, built, and validated.
- **Continuous Deployment (CD)**: Automates the deployment of validated models or code to production environments after passing all stages of testing and validation, ensuring seamless integration into the existing system.

In ML, the CI/CD process handles not only code but also data, models, and configurations, making the workflow more complex than traditional software projects.

2. Components of a CI/CD Pipeline for Machine Learning

1. **Source Control and Versioning**:
   - Track code, datasets, and models using version control tools such as **Git** for code and **DVC** for data and model versioning.
2. **Automated Testing**:
   - Test the integrity of your ML models through unit tests, integration tests, and data validation checks.
3. **Model Training and Validation**:
   - Re-train models with the latest data, and validate performance metrics before pushing them to production.
4. **Continuous Deployment**:
   - Automatically deploy trained models to production environments (e.g., Kubernetes clusters, cloud platforms) after passing all tests.
5. **Monitoring and Feedback Loops**:
   - Monitor models for performance drifts and trigger retraining workflows when necessary.

3. CI/CD Pipeline for ML: Example Workflow

Step 1: Code and Data Versioning

Using Git for code versioning and tools like **DVC (Data Version Control)** for tracking changes in datasets, models, and parameters ensures reproducibility.

Example: Using DVC to version control data

dvcinit

dvc add data/training_data.csv

git add data/.gitignore data/training_data.csv.dvc

git commit -m "Add training dataset"

Step 2: Automated Testing

Implement automated testing to check the integrity of data, code, and models. You can use testing frameworks like **pytest** and integrate it into the pipeline.

Run pytest to test ML code

pytest tests/test_model.py

Step 3: Model Training and Validation

Define a pipeline that automatically trains the model when there's a change in the dataset or hyperparameters, and validate it against a test set. Tools like **MLflow** can help track experiments.

Example using MLflow for tracking experiments

mlflowrun . --entry-point train --experiment-id 1

Step 4: Model Deployment

After testing and validation, models are deployed to production automatically using tools like **Kubernetes** and **Docker**.

- **Docker** is used to containerize the model for reproducibility, and **Kubernetes** orchestrates the deployment of the containerized model.

Dockerfile Example:

FROM python:3.8

WORKDIR /app

COPY requirements.txt .

RUN pip install -r requirements.txt

COPY . /app

```
CMD ["python", "app.py"]
```

Kubernetes Deployment Example:

```
apiVersion: apps/v1

kind: Deployment

metadata:

  name: ml-model-deployment

spec:

  replicas: 2

  selector:

matchLabels:

    app: ml-model

  template:

   metadata:

    labels:

      app: ml-model

   spec:

    containers:

    - name: ml-model

      image: registry.example.com/ml-model:latest

      ports:
```

- containerPort: 5000

Step 5: Monitoring

After deployment, the model needs continuous monitoring to track its performance. If the model drifts, feedback loops can automatically trigger re-training.

4. Tools for CI/CD in Machine Learning

- **Git/DVC**: Version control for code and datasets.
- **Jenkins**: Automates building, testing, and deploying machine learning models.
- **MLflow**: Tracks experiments, hyperparameters, and model performance.
- **Docker**: Containerizes models to ensure consistency across environments.
- **Kubernetes**: Orchestrates model deployment and scaling.
- **Prometheus/Grafana**: Used for monitoring model performance in production.

5. Example CI/CD Pipeline Using Jenkins

Here's a basic Jenkins pipeline for an ML project:

```
pipeline {

    agent any

    stages {

stage('Clone Repository') {

        steps {

            git 'https://github.com/your-ml-repo.git'

        }
```

```
        }
stage('Install Dependencies') {

        steps {

sh 'pip install -r requirements.txt'

        }

    }
stage('Run Tests') {

        steps {

sh 'pytest tests/'

        }

    }
stage('Train Model') {

        steps {

sh 'python train_model.py'

        }

    }
stage('Build Docker Image') {

        steps {

            script {

dockerImage = docker.build("mlops_model:${env.BUILD_ID}")
```

```
                }

            }

        }

stage('Deploy to Kubernetes') {

        steps {

sh 'kubectl apply -f k8s-deployment.yaml'

                }

            }

        }

}
```

6. Benefits of CI/CD for Machine Learning Projects

- **Automation**: Automates the repetitive tasks of testing, training, and deployment.
- **Reproducibility**: Ensures that code, data, and models are version-controlled and easily reproducible.
- **Faster Time to Market**: Continuous deployment allows you to quickly push new models into production, reducing the time between development and release.
- **Scalability**: CI/CD pipelines can scale the deployment of machine learning models across various platforms and environments seamlessly.

Conclusion

Building CI/CD pipelines for machine learning projects not only automates the process of code integration and deployment but also addresses the unique challenges that come with the machine learning lifecycle, such as model versioning, monitoring, and retraining. By incorporating tools like Kubernetes, Jenkins,

Docker, and DVC, organizations can streamline ML operations and ensure reliable and efficient deployment of models to production.

Automating Data Pipelines for ML Workflows

Automating data pipelines is a critical aspect of the MLOps (Machine Learning Operations) lifecycle, ensuring seamless, efficient, and consistent data handling across all stages of an ML project—from data ingestion to model deployment. By automating these pipelines, organizations can improve data reliability, speed up model development, and enable continuous integration and deployment of machine learning models.

1. What is a Data Pipeline?

A data pipeline is a series of data processing steps, often automated, that move raw data from various sources to a destination where it can be used for analysis or machine learning. Data pipelines are crucial in transforming, cleaning, and validating data to ensure its quality before being fed into machine learning models.

2. Why Automate Data Pipelines?

- **Efficiency**: Automation reduces manual intervention, ensuring that data is always up-to-date for training and model development.
- **Reproducibility**: By automating data collection, cleaning, and processing, the pipeline ensures consistency across different runs, leading to more reliable and reproducible models.
- **Scalability**: Automated data pipelines can handle large volumes of data, scale horizontally, and integrate multiple data sources seamlessly.

- **Error Reduction**: Automation minimizes human error in repetitive data tasks like cleaning, transformation, and ingestion.

3. Components of an Automated Data Pipeline

1. **Data Ingestion**: Collects data from various sources like databases, APIs, and cloud storage.
   - **Tools**: Apache Kafka, Apache NiFi, AWS Glue

Example: Automatically ingest data from an API endpoint into a storage bucket.

```
import requests

import json

import boto3



# Fetch data from API

response = requests.get('https://api.example.com/data')

data = response.json()



# Save to AWS S3 bucket

s3 = boto3.client('s3')

s3.put_object(Bucket='ml-dataset',          Key='data.json',
Body=json.dumps(data))
```

2. **Data Preprocessing and Cleaning**: Transform raw data into a usable format, handle missing values, normalize features, and remove noise.

- **Tools**: Apache Airflow, Python (Pandas, NumPy)

Example: Automate missing value handling and normalization using Python.

import pandas as pd

from sklearn.preprocessing import StandardScaler

Load data

df = pd.read_csv('data.csv')

Fill missing values

df.fillna(df.mean(), inplace=True)

Normalize features

scaler = StandardScaler()

df[['feature1', 'feature2']] = scaler.fit_transform(df[['feature1', 'feature2']])

Save cleaned data

df.to_csv('cleaned_data.csv', index=False)

3. **Data Validation**: Ensure that the data meets the required quality standards before training models.

- **Tools**: Great Expectations, TFDV (TensorFlow Data Validation)

Example: Validate data schema and check for anomalies using Great Expectations.

```
import great_expectations as ge



# Load the data

df = ge.read_csv('cleaned_data.csv')



# Validate schema

expectations                                =
df.expect_column_values_to_be_in_set('column_name',
['expected_value1', 'expected_value2'])



# Validate data type

df.expect_column_values_to_match_strftime_format('dat
e_column', '%Y-%m-%d')
```

4. **Feature Engineering**: Automate the generation of new features that improve model performance.

- **Tools**: Python (Scikit-learn, Featuretools), DBT (Data Build Tool)

Example: Automate feature engineering with **Featuretools**.

```
import featuretools as ft
```

```
# Load data

es = ft.EntitySet(id="customer_data")

es.entity_from_dataframe(entity_id="customers",
dataframe=df, index="customer_id")


# Automatically generate features

feature_matrix,    feature_defs    =    ft.dfs(entityset=es,
target_entity="customers")
```

5. **Data Storage**: Store raw, processed, and feature-engineered data for model training and future analysis.

• **Tools**: AWS S3, Google Cloud Storage, HDFS

Example: Automatically store processed data in a cloud storage service like S3

```
import boto3


# Upload cleaned data to S3

s3 = boto3.client('s3')

s3.upload_file('cleaned_data.csv',           'my-bucket',
'data/cleaned_data.csv')
```

6. **Orchestration**: Manage the workflow and ensure tasks in the data pipeline are executed in sequence or parallel as needed.

• **Tools**: Apache Airflow, Prefect, Luigi

Example: Create a pipeline workflow in **Apache Airflow**.

```python
from airflow import DAG

from airflow.operators.python_operator import PythonOperator

from datetime import datetime


# Define the pipeline

def ingest_data():

    # Ingestion logic

    pass


def preprocess_data():

    # Preprocessing logic

    pass


def validate_data():

    # Validation logic

    pass


default_args = {'start_date': datetime(2023, 1, 1)}

dag = DAG('ml_pipeline', default_args=default_args, schedule_interval='@daily')
```

```
ingest_task   =   PythonOperator(task_id='ingest_data',
python_callable=ingest_data, dag=dag)

preprocess_task                              =
PythonOperator(task_id='preprocess_data',
python_callable=preprocess_data, dag=dag)

validate_task = PythonOperator(task_id='validate_data',
python_callable=validate_data, dag=dag)


# Task dependencies

ingest_task>>preprocess_task>>validate_task
```

4. Tools for Automating Data Pipelines

- **Apache Airflow**: A popular workflow orchestrator to schedule, automate, and monitor data pipelines.
- **AWS Glue**: A fully managed ETL service for data preparation and integration in cloud environments.
- **DVC (Data Version Control)**: A tool that tracks data and models version control alongside the source code.
- **Prefect**: An orchestration tool with a modern approach to data pipeline automation.
- **Great Expectations**: A tool for automated data validation and testing.

5. Benefits of Automated Data Pipelines

- **Speed and Efficiency**: Automated pipelines ensure that data processing tasks are handled quickly and efficiently without manual intervention.
- **Reproducibility**: Every step in the pipeline is logged, making it easier to reproduce results and share workflows.

- **Scalability**: As data grows, automated pipelines can scale without the need for significant changes in infrastructure or code.
- **Consistency**: Automated pipelines enforce consistent data processing steps, ensuring the reliability of the data.
- **Reduced Human Error**: By eliminating manual steps, data pipelines reduce the risk of human errors in data handling.

6. Challenges of Automating Data Pipelines

- **Data Quality Issues**: Automatically ingesting large volumes of data increases the risk of ingesting bad or corrupted data.
- **Complexity**: The complexity of managing dependencies between tasks, such as feature engineering, model training, and monitoring, can increase.
- **Infrastructure Requirements**: Building automated pipelines at scale often requires robust infrastructure that can handle the load of multiple workflows running in parallel.

Conclusion

Automating data pipelines is essential for creating efficient, scalable, and reproducible ML workflows. By utilizing tools like Apache Airflow, DVC, and AWS Glue, teams can reduce manual efforts, ensure data quality, and create a seamless flow from data ingestion to model deployment. Automated pipelines enable teams to focus more on model development and tuning, while the data preparation process becomes faster, consistent, and reliable.

Chapter-5 Data Versioning and Management

Introduction to Data Versioning

Data versioning is a critical practice in Machine Learning Operations (MLOps), ensuring that the various stages of a machine learning workflow, including data preparation, model training, and deployment, are repeatable, traceable, and reproducible. Just as code versioning tools like Git enable teams to track changes in software development, data versioning helps track changes to datasets and models over time, allowing for better control and understanding of how the data evolves.

1. What is Data Versioning?

Data versioning refers to the process of systematically tracking and managing different versions of datasets used in machine learning projects. As models rely heavily on data for training, testing, and validation, it is crucial to record and track how datasets change over time to ensure that experiments can be reproduced, results are reliable, and models are deployed with the correct data.

- **Core Concept**: Maintain a history of changes to data, similar to how software version control systems keep track of code changes.

2. Why is Data Versioning Important in MLOps?

- **Reproducibility**: It ensures that the same dataset used for model training can be retrieved later to reproduce the results.
- **Traceability**: Provides an audit trail of which data versions were used in different stages of the pipeline (development, testing, production).
- **Collaboration**: Facilitates collaboration among teams by ensuring everyone has access to the correct version of the data.
- **Regulatory Compliance**: In regulated industries, data versioning is essential for compliance, as it helps demonstrate which data was used for specific models.

3. Challenges Without Data Versioning

- **Data Drift**: Over time, the underlying data can change, which may lead to different model outputs if data changes are not tracked.
- **Model Inconsistencies**: When models are retrained, using a different dataset version without tracking can result in inconsistencies and unreliable model performance.
- **Lack of Experiment Tracking**: Without versioning, it's difficult to correlate model performance to specific datasets, making it hard to analyze past experiments.

4. Tools for Data Versioning

Several tools and platforms help manage data versioning, especially in machine learning projects:

- **DVC (Data Version Control)**: A popular open-source tool that integrates with Git to provide data versioning and model management.

Initialize a DVC project

dvcinit

Track a dataset

dvc add dataset.csv

Commit dataset version

git add dataset.csv.dvc .gitignore

git commit -m "Track dataset version"

- **Pachyderm**: A data versioning tool that uses Git-like semantics for large-scale datasets.
- **MLFlow**: Although primarily used for experiment tracking, MLFlow can be integrated with data versioning tools to track data changes.

5. Best Practices for Data Versioning in MLOps

1. **Track Raw and Processed Data**: Always version both raw and transformed datasets to ensure you can reproduce the preprocessing pipeline.
2. **Integrate with CI/CD**: Incorporate data versioning as part of your Continuous Integration/Continuous Deployment (CI/CD) pipeline to automate the tracking of data changes.
3. **Automated Data Versioning**: Use automation tools to ensure that each new dataset version is automatically captured and stored.

4. **Version Metadata**: In addition to datasets, track metadata like the schema, preprocessing methods, and feature engineering techniques used at each version.

6. Benefits of Data Versioning

- **Model Reliability**: Versioning allows you to track exactly which data a model was trained on, ensuring reliability in production.
- **Experiment Reproducibility**: By pairing data versioning with model and code versioning, you can recreate past experiments with exact conditions.
- **Simplified Rollbacks**: In case of errors or issues with a model in production, data versioning allows you to roll back to a previous version of the dataset.
- **Collaboration Across Teams**: Teams working on different parts of the pipeline can easily share and access specific data versions.

7. Real-World Use Case of Data Versioning

In large-scale machine learning projects, such as autonomous driving systems, data versioning plays a critical role in managing the immense volumes of training data. Each new version of the training dataset must be tracked, as models are constantly retrained with updated data to adapt to new conditions on the road. Without proper versioning, it would be impossible to ensure that a model deployed to a vehicle fleet is trained on the right dataset.

Conclusion

Data versioning is an essential practice in MLOps that ensures machine learning projects remain reproducible, reliable, and scalable. By using tools like DVC and integrating versioning into CI/CD pipelines, teams can keep track of every data change, ensuring that models are always trained and deployed with the right data. This practice not only helps in maintaining model accuracy and integrity but also fosters collaboration and compliance in ML projects.

Tools for Data Version Control

Data version control tools are essential in MLOps workflows for tracking and managing different versions of datasets, ensuring reproducibility, traceability, and collaboration. Here are some of the most popular tools used for data versioning in machine learning projects:

1. DVC (Data Version Control)

Overview: DVC is an open-source tool designed to help data scientists and machine learning engineers manage datasets, code, and models with Git-like workflows. DVC tracks large files, datasets, and machine learning models while allowing teams to version control all project assets alongside code.

- **Key Features**:
    - Seamless integration with Git for managing datasets and model files.
    - Remote storage support (S3, Google Drive, Azure Blob Storage) for versioning large datasets.
    - Tracks data dependencies and outputs, making pipelines reproducible.
    - Simple commands for adding, versioning, and pulling datasets.
- **Example Workflow**:

Initialize DVC project

dvcinit

Add a dataset to version control

dvc add dataset.csv

```
# Commit dataset metadata and track changes

git add dataset.csv.dvc .gitignore

git commit -m "Version control dataset"
```

```
# Push the dataset to remote storage (e.g., S3, Google Drive)

dvc remote add -d myremote s3://bucket/path

dvc push
```

- **Use Case**: DVC is ideal for teams that already use Git for code versioning and want to manage large datasets or machine learning models in a similar workflow. It provides easy integration with CI/CD pipelines and enables reproducibility by versioning the data and model artifacts.

2. Pachyderm

Overview: Pachyderm is a data platform that combines data versioning with pipeline management, enabling data-driven workflows with Git-like functionality. It is built for handling large-scale data in distributed environments and integrates well with machine learning workflows.

- **Key Features**:
  - Data versioning at scale with Git-like commits for datasets.
  - Automates data pipelines with integrated pipeline management.
  - Supports both structured and unstructured data.
  - Provides fine-grained control over data lineage and version tracking.
- **Example Workflow**:

Create a Pachyderm repository for data

pachctl create repo mydata

Commit a new version of the dataset

pachctl put file mydata@master:/data.csv -f /path/to/dataset.csv

View the data history (commits)

pachctl list commit mydata

Create a pipeline that processes the data

pachctl create pipeline -f pipeline.json

- **Use Case**: Pachyderm is useful for data teams managing large, distributed datasets and building complex machine learning pipelines. It is particularly well-suited for teams working on big data projects, as it scales efficiently and offers powerful pipeline orchestration.

3. MLflow

Overview: While primarily known for experiment tracking, MLflow also allows for the management of datasets and model artifacts alongside machine learning experiments. MLflow integrates with data versioning tools like DVC, enabling teams to track which datasets were used for each experiment and model version.

- **Key Features**:

- o Tracks datasets and models used in experiments.
- o Integrates with tools like DVC for data versioning.
- o Provides logging and comparison of experiments, including data changes.
- o Supports multiple remote storage backends for managing large datasets.
- **Example Workflow**:

import mlflow

Start an MLflow run and log dataset details

with mlflow.start_run():

mlflow.log_param("dataset_version", "v1.0")

mlflow.log_artifact("dataset.csv")

Track the model version along with the dataset used

mlflow.log_model(model, "model_path")

- **Use Case**: MLflow is well-suited for teams that want to track not only their datasets but also their entire machine learning lifecycle, from data preparation to model deployment. It's an excellent option for experiment tracking with dataset versioning.

4. LakeFS

Overview: LakeFS is an open-source data versioning platform designed for large-scale data lakes. It provides Git-like operations for versioning data stored in cloud storage, such as

S3, making it a great fit for organizations that manage big data projects in data lakes.

- **Key Features**:
  - Supports large-scale data versioning with minimal overhead.
  - Git-like branching and committing functionality for datasets.
  - Provides snapshots and data lineage for reproducible workflows.
  - Integrates with modern data lakes (S3, GCS) and ETL tools.
- **Example Workflow**:

Create a new branch for versioning

lakefs branch create mydata

Commit new dataset to the branch

lakefs commit mydata -m "Add new dataset version"

Merge changes to the master branch

lakefs merge mydata master

- **Use Case**: LakeFS is ideal for organizations managing large-scale data lakes where tracking and versioning of big data is necessary. It's commonly used in industries like finance, healthcare, and retail for data science and machine learning projects.

5. Quilt

Overview: Quilt is a data management tool that provides version control for datasets, enabling teams to version, share, and reuse data. It integrates with S3 for cloud storage, making it a scalable solution for managing large datasets in cloud environments.

- **Key Features**:
    - o Simple version control for datasets with S3 integration.
    - o Enables data discovery and reuse with powerful search functionality.
    - o Automates data lineage tracking and sharing across teams.
    - o Supports both structured and unstructured data formats.
- **Example Workflow**:

```
# Upload a dataset to Quilt and version it

quilt push my-dataset
```

```
# Check the dataset's version history

quilt log my-dataset
```

```
# Pull a specific version of the dataset

quilt pull my-dataset:v1.0
```

- **Use Case**: Quilt is great for teams managing datasets in cloud environments like AWS. It provides easy version control and data discovery, making it a good option for managing and sharing datasets across data science and machine learning teams.

Conclusion

Data version control is an essential component of any robust MLOps pipeline. Tools like DVC, Pachyderm, MLflow, LakeFS, and Quilt enable teams to effectively manage datasets, ensure reproducibility, and streamline collaboration across machine learning workflows. By incorporating data versioning into your MLOps practices, you can ensure traceable, scalable, and reliable machine learning models.

Data Quality and Monitoring in MLOps

Overview: In MLOps, ensuring the quality of data and monitoring its changes over time is crucial for building robust and reliable machine learning models. Data quality refers to the accuracy, consistency, completeness, and timeliness of data, while monitoring helps identify potential data drift, quality issues, or anomalies that could degrade model performance.

1. Importance of Data Quality in Machine Learning

- **Accuracy**: The data must represent real-world values and events correctly. Inaccurate data can lead to incorrect predictions.
- **Consistency**: Data should be consistent across different sources and periods. Inconsistent data can create confusion in training models.
- **Completeness**: Incomplete data can reduce model performance or lead to incorrect interpretations.
- **Timeliness**: Up-to-date data ensures that models reflect current trends and events, particularly important in fast-changing domains.

2. Data Quality Dimensions

- **Data Completeness**: Monitoring whether all necessary data fields are filled in without missing values.
- **Data Accuracy**: Ensuring that the data accurately represents the reality or the process it's meant to model.

- **Data Consistency**: Checking whether data remains uniform across different datasets or over time.
- **Data Timeliness**: Ensuring that the data used is relevant and up to date for the context in which it is used.
- **Data Uniqueness**: Verifying that there are no duplicate records in the dataset.

3. Monitoring Data Quality Using MLOps Tools

- **Data Validation**: Automatically checks datasets for missing values, incorrect data types, and anomalies before feeding them into machine learning pipelines.
- **Data Profiling**: Analyzing datasets for statistical properties like distributions, null values, and outliers to ensure that data is within expected ranges.
- **Data Drift Detection**: Using monitoring tools to identify shifts in the data distribution that can degrade model performance over time.

4. Tools for Data Quality Monitoring in MLOps

a. Great Expectations

Overview: Great Expectations is an open-source tool for validating, documenting, and profiling data to ensure data quality.

- **Key Features**:
  - Automatically generates data validation tests based on expectations.
  - Detects data anomalies, missing values, and schema mismatches.
  - Provides a human-readable data quality report.

Example:

import great_expectations as ge

```
# Load dataset

df = ge.from_pandas(data)


# Define expectations

df.expect_column_values_to_not_be_null('column_name')

df.expect_column_values_to_be_in_set('column_name',
['value1', 'value2'])


# Validate data

results = df.validate()


# Check results

print(results)
```

b. TFX (TensorFlow Extended)

Overview: TFX is an end-to-end platform for deploying production ML pipelines, which includes built-in tools for data validation and monitoring.

- **Key Features**:
    - o Data validation during pipeline execution.
    - o Automatically detects anomalies and schema changes.
    - o Scalable for large datasets in distributed environments.

Example:

```
from tfx.components import StatisticsGen, ExampleValidator

from tfx.utils.dsl_utils import csv_input


# Load data

example_gen = csv_input(data_dir='path_to_data')


# Generate statistics

statistics_gen = StatisticsGen(examples=example_gen)


# Validate statistics

example_validator = ExampleValidator(statistics=statistics_gen)
```

5. Continuous Monitoring for Data Drift and Quality

Data Drift: Occurs when the statistical properties of the input data change over time, causing the model's performance to degrade.

- **Tools for Data Drift Monitoring**:
  - **Evidently AI**: Open-source tool for monitoring data and model performance, tracking data drift, and generating reports.
  - **WhyLabs**: Platform for real-time monitoring of data pipelines, detecting anomalies, and ensuring data integrity.

Example: Using **Evidently AI** for data drift detection.

```
import evidently
```

```
from evidently.test_suite import TestSuite

from evidently.tests import TestDataDrift


# Create a test suite for data drift

data_drift_test = TestSuite(tests=[TestDataDrift()])


# Compare current and baseline datasets

data_drift_test.run(current_data=current_df,
reference_data=baseline_df)

data_drift_test.show()
```

6. Monitoring Model and Data Pipelines

Monitoring the data pipelines is as crucial as monitoring the model. Tools like **Prometheus**, **Grafana**, and **MLflow** are commonly used to monitor machine learning and data pipelines.

- **Prometheus**: Open-source system for monitoring and alerting, often used in MLOps to track metrics like data quality and pipeline health.
- **Grafana**: Visualization tool that integrates with Prometheus and allows for creating dashboards to track data and model performance in real-time.

7. Best Practices for Data Quality and Monitoring in MLOps

- **Automate Data Validation**: Automate data checks and anomaly detection in the pipeline to avoid manual interventions.
- **Set Alerts for Drift**: Establish alerts for when data drift is detected, so the team can quickly address potential issues.

- **Track Data Lineage**: Ensure traceability of data transformations and ensure that changes are monitored and tracked for future audits.
- **Use Version Control**: Maintain version control for datasets similar to how code is versioned, ensuring repeatability.

Conclusion

Ensuring data quality and monitoring for changes over time is an essential part of the MLOps lifecycle. By implementing the right tools and practices, teams can prevent model degradation, maintain high performance, and scale their machine learning solutions efficiently. Automated monitoring and validation frameworks such as Great Expectations and TFX ensure data quality, while tools like Evidently AI help detect data drift in real-time.

Handling Data Drift and Concept Drift in MLOps

Overview: In machine learning systems, maintaining model performance over time is crucial. However, models often encounter issues when the underlying data distribution or the relationships between input features and the target variable change. These changes are known as **data drift** and **concept drift**, and if left unchecked, they can lead to poor model performance. Managing these drifts is a key challenge in MLOps, requiring continuous monitoring and adaptation.

1. What is Data Drift?

- **Definition**: Data drift refers to the change in the distribution of input data over time. It occurs when the statistical properties of the data, such as mean, variance, or distribution, shift from what was observed during training.

- **Types of Data Drift**:
  - ○ **Covariate Shift**: When the distribution of the independent variables (features) changes but the relationship between features and the target remains the same.
  - ○ **Prior Probability Shift**: When the distribution of the target variable changes, but the conditional distribution of the features given the target remains constant.

Example: A model trained to predict customer churn based on historical data might experience data drift if new customer behaviors emerge due to external factors like market changes or promotions.

2. What is Concept Drift?

- **Definition**: Concept drift refers to changes in the underlying relationship between the input features and the target variable. This means that even if the input data stays the same, the way it influences the output may change over time.
- **Types of Concept Drift**:
  - ○ **Sudden Drift**: The target distribution changes abruptly, leading to an immediate drop in model performance.
  - ○ **Gradual Drift**: The target distribution changes slowly over time, and the model performance gradually declines.
  - ○ **Recurrent Drift**: Patterns in the data change periodically (e.g., seasonal changes in customer behavior).

Example: In a stock price prediction model, the relationship between certain economic indicators and stock prices may change due to unforeseen events like a financial crisis.

3. Detecting Data Drift and Concept Drift

To handle drifts effectively, you first need to detect them using various techniques:

- **Statistical Tests**:
    - o **Kolmogorov-Smirnov Test**: Used to check if two datasets (training and current data) follow the same distribution.
    - o **Chi-Square Test**: Compares categorical features to detect distributional changes.
    - o **KL Divergence**: Measures how one probability distribution diverges from a second reference distribution.

Example: Using a statistical test to detect drift.

```
from scipy.stats import ks_2samp
```

```
# Detecting data drift for a numerical feature
```

```
statistic,    p_value    =    ks_2samp(train_data['feature'],
current_data['feature'])
```

```
if p_value< 0.05:
```

```
print("Data drift detected")
```

- **Model-Based Monitoring**:
    - o Train a secondary model to predict the probability that the data comes from the training set or the new set. If the model can differentiate between the two, it suggests drift has occurred.

4. Handling Data Drift and Concept Drift

Once data drift or concept drift is detected, there are several strategies to mitigate their effects:

a. Retraining the Model

- **Periodic Retraining**: Retrain the model on recent data at regular intervals to adapt to gradual changes in data distribution or relationships.
- **Triggered Retraining**: Retrain the model only when a significant drift is detected, which optimizes resources and avoids unnecessary training.

Example: Automating retraining with data drift detection.

if p_value< 0.05:

  # Data drift detected, retrain the model

new_model = retrain_model(current_data)

b. Incremental Learning

- In cases of gradual drift, incremental learning techniques can be employed to continuously update the model with new data without a full retraining process.

Tools: **River** is a library designed for online learning, where models are updated incrementally with new data points.

c. Weighted Training

- Assign higher weights to recent data points when retraining, allowing the model to adapt more quickly to changes in data distribution while still considering older data.

d. Model Stacking

- Use an ensemble of models trained on different time periods. If concept drift occurs, the ensemble will be more robust than a single model trained on outdated data.

e. Concept Drift Mitigation

- **Windowing**: Use a sliding window of the most recent data for training, ensuring that the model only learns from the latest trends.
- **Adaptive Models**: Implement models that can adjust their internal parameters based on new data without full retraining, such as decision trees that grow dynamically as new data is introduced.

5. Tools for Data Drift and Concept Drift Detection

a. **Evidently AI**

- A popular tool for monitoring data drift, concept drift, and generating detailed reports on the performance of machine learning models in production environments.

Example: Using Evidently AI to detect data drift.

```
import evidently

from evidently.test_suite import TestSuite

from evidently.tests import TestDataDrift


# Set up data drift test suite

drift_suite = TestSuite(tests=[TestDataDrift()])

drift_suite.run(reference_data=train_data,
current_data=current_data)

drift_suite.show()
```

b. **Fiddler AI**

- A platform that provides AI model performance monitoring, including features to detect data drift and model drift.

c. **WhyLabs**

- WhyLabs offers real-time monitoring of data and model performance, focusing on detecting and explaining data drift and concept drift in production.

6. Best Practices for Handling Drift in MLOps

- **Monitor Continuously**: Regularly monitor data and model performance to detect drift as early as possible.
- **Use Alerts**: Set up alerts for when drift is detected, enabling quick action such as retraining or recalibrating the model.
- **Implement Version Control**: Keep track of different versions of the model and data to ensure that drifts can be understood in the context of historical changes.
- **Establish Feedback Loops**: Integrate real-time feedback from the model's performance in production to understand how drift affects outputs.

Conclusion

Handling data drift and concept drift is critical in maintaining the performance of machine learning models in production. By implementing robust monitoring systems and strategies for retraining, updating, or adapting models, organizations can minimize the risk of model degradation and ensure that their machine learning solutions remain effective over time. With the use of tools like Evidently AI and WhyLabs, detecting and responding to drift becomes a streamlined process, allowing MLOps teams to exceed expectations in real-time environments.

Chapter-6 Model Development and Experiment Tracking

Introduction to Experiment Tracking

Experiment tracking in MLOps is essential for organizing, comparing, and managing machine learning experiments. It enables data scientists and ML engineers to log every detail of their ML model development process, such as model parameters, metrics, training results, and artifacts (e.g., model binaries and logs). Experiment tracking tools streamline the iterative nature of model training, allowing teams to understand what has been tried, which parameters or configurations worked best, and why certain models outperformed others. This practice is foundational to reproducibility, collaboration, and deployment in production ML systems.

Here's a detailed guide to experiment tracking in MLOps, including code examples using tools like **MLflow** and **Weights & Biases**.

Why Experiment Tracking is Important

- **Reproducibility**: Ensures that experiments can be recreated exactly, even months later.
- **Comparability**: Makes it easy to compare different versions and configurations.
- **Collaboration**: Team members can review each other's experiments and findings.
- **Efficiency**: Saves time by avoiding repeated efforts and quickly identifying effective configurations.

Common Experiment Tracking Tools

1. **MLflow**: An open-source platform for managing the ML lifecycle, including experimentation, reproducibility, and deployment.
2. **Weights & Biases (W&B)**: A collaborative platform for experiment tracking, versioning, and visualization.
3. **Comet**: Provides experiment tracking, visualizations, and hyperparameter tuning with an emphasis on collaboration.
4. **Neptune**: Offers experiment tracking with extensive logging and visualization capabilities.

In this guide, we'll focus on **MLflow** and **Weights & Biases (W&B)** to illustrate experiment tracking with examples.

Experiment Tracking with MLflow

Installation

To start using MLflow, install it using pip:

pip install mlflow

Setting Up Experiment Tracking with MLflow

MLflow allows you to create an experiment, log various parameters, metrics, and artifacts, and compare runs. Here's an example workflow using MLflow.

Code Example

```python
import mlflow

import mlflow.sklearn

from sklearn.ensemble import RandomForestClassifier

from sklearn.model_selection import train_test_split

from sklearn.datasets import load_iris

from sklearn.metrics import accuracy_score


# Load sample data

data = load_iris()

X_train, X_test, y_train, y_test = train_test_split(data.data,
data.target, test_size=0.3, random_state=42)


# Set up experiment

mlflow.set_experiment("Iris Classification Experiment")


with mlflow.start_run(run_name="RandomForest Model"):
    # Define model parameters
    n_estimators = 100
    max_depth = 5
    mlflow.log_param("n_estimators", n_estimators)
```

```
mlflow.log_param("max_depth", max_depth)


# Train the model

model = RandomForestClassifier(n_estimators=n_estimators,
max_depth=max_depth, random_state=42)

model.fit(X_train, y_train)


# Make predictions

predictions = model.predict(X_test)

accuracy = accuracy_score(y_test, predictions)


# Log metrics

mlflow.log_metric("accuracy", accuracy)


# Log the model

mlflow.sklearn.log_model(model, "random_forest_model")


# Log the model as an artifact

mlflow.log_artifact("model.pkl")


print("Experiment tracked in MLflow")
```

Explanation

- **Parameters**: mlflow.log_param records the model's hyperparameters, allowing us to track variations.
- **Metrics**: mlflow.log_metric logs metrics like accuracy, loss, or precision.

- **Model Logging**: mlflow.sklearn.log_model saves the model artifact, which can be retrieved later.
- **Artifacts**: Any additional files, like a pickled model or configuration files, can be stored using mlflow.log_artifact.

Viewing Experiments in the MLflow UI

To view your experiment:

1. Run the MLflow tracking server using

   mlflow ui

2. Open http://localhost:5000 in your browser. You'll see an interface displaying your experiments, parameters, metrics, and logged artifacts.

Experiment Tracking with Weights & Biases (W&B)

Weights & Biases (W&B) is a powerful experiment tracking tool with extensive logging, comparison, and visualization features. Here's how to set up experiment tracking with W&B.

Installation

To use W&B, install it using pip and set up an account on the W&B website:

    pip install wandb

Code Example with Weights & Biases

import wandb

from sklearn.ensemble import RandomForestClassifier

```
from sklearn.model_selection import train_test_split

from sklearn.datasets import load_iris

from sklearn.metrics import accuracy_score


# Initialize a new W&B run

wandb.init(project="iris_classification")


# Load sample data

data = load_iris()

X_train, X_test, y_train, y_test = train_test_split(data.data,
data.target, test_size=0.3, random_state=42)


# Define model parameters

config = {

    "n_estimators": 100,

    "max_depth": 5,

}

wandb.config.update(config)


# Train the model

model                                                       =
RandomForestClassifier(n_estimators=config["n_estimators"],
max_depth=config["max_depth"], random_state=42)

model.fit(X_train, y_train)


# Make predictions
```

```
predictions = model.predict(X_test)

accuracy = accuracy_score(y_test, predictions)


# Log metrics to W&B

wandb.log({"accuracy": accuracy})


# Save the model and log as an artifact

model_path = "random_forest_model.pkl"

with open(model_path, "wb") as f:

    pickle.dump(model, f)

wandb.save(model_path)


print("Experiment tracked in Weights & Biases")
```

Explanation

- **Initialization**: wandb.init() initializes a new run, and project specifies the project name.
- **Parameter Logging**: The model's hyperparameters are logged in wandb.config.
- **Metric Logging**: Model performance metrics (e.g., accuracy) are logged using wandb.log.
- **Model Artifact Logging**: Save the model and upload it as an artifact for retrieval and comparison in the W&B dashboard.

Viewing Experiments in the W&B UI

1. Run the code, and it will automatically open a session on the W&B web interface, where you can view all experiment details, parameters, metrics, and logged artifacts.

2. Go to your W&B dashboard, where you'll see a timeline of experiments, comparisons, and insights.

Advanced Experiment Tracking Techniques

1. **Hyperparameter Sweeps**: Both MLflow and W&B support hyperparameter sweeps to optimize model performance across a grid or random search of hyperparameters.
   o In W&B, wandb.sweep() allows you to define a sweep configuration to run multiple experiments with different hyperparameter settings.
2. **Experiment Versioning**: Experiment tracking tools version each run, allowing you to revert to a previous model configuration, compare results, and reproduce past experiments.
3. **Model Lineage Tracking**: By logging model artifacts and metadata, you can track model lineage, linking each experiment to the data version, parameters, and code used for training.
4. **Advanced Visualizations**: W&B provides advanced visualizations, including loss curves, confusion matrices, and feature importance, for more in-depth analysis of model performance.

Comparison of MLflow and W&B

Feature	MLflow	Weights & Biases (W&B)
Setup Complexity	Easy to set up locally	Requires W&B account
UI/Visualization	Basic experiment tracking UI	Advanced, customizable charts
Parameter Tracking	Yes	Yes
Hyperparameter Sweeps	Basic	Extensive sweep configuration

Feature	MLflow	Weights & Biases (W&B)
Artifact Management	Supports artifacts	Supports artifacts and files
Collaborative Features	Limited	Strong collaborative tools
Cloud Integration	Compatible with cloud storage	Integrates with cloud services

Conclusion

Experiment tracking is essential in MLOps for managing model versions, parameters, and results. Tools like MLflow and Weights & Biases offer robust solutions for logging, comparing, and managing ML experiments, enabling reproducibility and collaboration. Experiment tracking not only optimizes the ML workflow but also makes the transition from development to production smoother, as models are tracked and validated effectively throughout their lifecycle.

Using experiment tracking, ML teams can confidently experiment, innovate, and deploy reliable models in production.

MLOps Experiment Tracking

In **MLOps**, **experiment tracking** is a key component for managing and organizing machine learning experiments. It enables teams to log model configurations, hyperparameters, metrics, and other relevant information throughout the model development lifecycle. This process ensures reproducibility, facilitates comparisons between different experiments, and helps with collaboration.

Here are some of the most popular **tools for experiment tracking** in MLOps, including **MLflow** and **Weights & Biases (W&B)**, along with example code for using them.

1. MLflow

MLflow is an open-source platform for managing the complete machine learning lifecycle. It allows users to track experiments, log parameters and metrics, and store models for future use. MLflow can be integrated with any machine learning framework and supports multiple deployment environments.

Key Features:

- **Experiment tracking**: Log and compare parameters, metrics, and models.
- **Model management**: Save, load, and deploy models.
- **Project packaging**: Organize code and dependencies in a consistent, reproducible way.

Installation:

pip install mlflow

Example Code with MLflow:

import mlflow

import mlflow.sklearn

from sklearn.ensemble import RandomForestClassifier

from sklearn.model_selection import train_test_split

from sklearn.datasets import load_iris

from sklearn.metrics import accuracy_score

Load Iris dataset

data = load_iris()

```
X_train, X_test, y_train, y_test = train_test_split(data.data,
data.target, test_size=0.3, random_state=42)


# Set up experiment

mlflow.set_experiment("Iris_Classification_Experiment")


with mlflow.start_run(run_name="RandomForest_Model_1"):
    # Log parameters
    n_estimators = 100
    max_depth = 5
    mlflow.log_param("n_estimators", n_estimators)
    mlflow.log_param("max_depth", max_depth)


    # Train the model
    model = RandomForestClassifier(n_estimators=n_estimators,
max_depth=max_depth, random_state=42)
    model.fit(X_train, y_train)


    # Make predictions
    predictions = model.predict(X_test)
    accuracy = accuracy_score(y_test, predictions)


    # Log metrics
    mlflow.log_metric("accuracy", accuracy)
```

```
# Save model as an artifact

mlflow.sklearn.log_model(model, "random_forest_model")


print("Experiment tracked in MLflow!")
```

Explanation:

- **mlflow.set_experiment**: Sets the experiment name where the run will be logged.
- **mlflow.start_run**: Starts a new run within the experiment, where all logs (parameters, metrics, models) will be captured.
- **mlflow.log_param**: Logs hyperparameters such as the number of estimators and max depth for the random forest.
- **mlflow.log_metric**: Logs metrics such as accuracy.
- **mlflow.sklearn.log_model**: Saves the trained model as an artifact.

Viewing the Experiment in MLflow UI

1. Start the MLflow UI server:

   ```
   mlflow ui
   ```

2. Open http://localhost:5000 in a browser to access the UI. You'll be able to see a detailed view of your experiments, including the logged parameters, metrics, and models.

2. Weights & Biases (W&B)

Weights & Biases (W&B) is a popular tool for experiment tracking, model versioning, and collaboration. It integrates easily with many machine learning frameworks and provides rich visualizations for metrics, hyperparameters, and model artifacts. W&B allows teams to collaborate on machine learning projects by sharing results and tracking experiments.

Key Features:

- **Real-time visualization**: View metrics, hyperparameters, and outputs in real-time.
- **Hyperparameter tuning**: Support for hyperparameter sweeps to automate model optimization.
- **Collaborative tools**: Share experiments, results, and artifacts with teams.

Installation:

```
pip install wandb
```

Example Code with W&B:

```
import wandb

from sklearn.ensemble import RandomForestClassifier

from sklearn.model_selection import train_test_split

from sklearn.datasets import load_iris

from sklearn.metrics import accuracy_score


# Initialize W&B project

wandb.init(project="iris_classification")


# Load Iris dataset

data = load_iris()

X_train, X_test, y_train, y_test = train_test_split(data.data, data.target, test_size=0.3, random_state=42)


# Define and log hyperparameters

config = {
```

```python
    "n_estimators": 100,

    "max_depth": 5

}

wandb.config.update(config)


# Train the model

model                                                    =
RandomForestClassifier(n_estimators=config["n_estimators"],
max_depth=config["max_depth"], random_state=42)

model.fit(X_train, y_train)


# Make predictions

predictions = model.predict(X_test)

accuracy = accuracy_score(y_test, predictions)


# Log metrics to W&B

wandb.log({"accuracy": accuracy})


# Save the model and log as an artifact

import pickle

model_path = "random_forest_model.pkl"

with open(model_path, "wb") as f:

    pickle.dump(model, f)

wandb.save(model_path)
```

```
print("Experiment tracked in Weights & Biases!")
```

Explanation:

- **wandb.init**: Initializes a new W&B run and sets the project name ("iris_classification").
- **wandb.config.update**: Logs hyperparameters like n_estimators and max_depth to W&B.
- **wandb.log**: Logs metrics like accuracy to the dashboard.
- **wandb.save**: Saves the model artifact, making it available for download and sharing.

Viewing the Experiment in W&B UI

1. After running the code, go to the W&B website and log into your account.
2. Navigate to your project ("iris_classification") to view experiment details such as hyperparameters, metrics, and artifacts.

3. Comparison of MLflow vs. Weights & Biases

Feature	MLflow	Weights & Biases (W&B)
Setup Complexity	Simple to set up, local and cloud	Requires W&B account
UI/Visualization	Basic, but functional	Rich and interactive
Parameter Logging	Yes	Yes
Metric Logging	Yes	Yes
Model Logging	Yes	Yes

Feature	MLflow	Weights & Biases (W&B)
Artifact Management	Yes	Yes
Collaborative Features	Limited	Strong collaboration tools
Hyperparameter Tuning	No (but can integrate with other tools like Optuna)	Yes (sweeps)
Cloud Integration	Can be configured for cloud-based backends	Native cloud integration

4. Advanced Features for Experiment Tracking

Hyperparameter Tuning:

Both **MLflow** and **W&B** support hyperparameter optimization. While MLflow requires integration with external libraries like **Optuna** or **Hyperopt**, **W&B** offers built-in support for hyperparameter sweeps, which automate the process of hyperparameter tuning.

- **W&B Sweeps**:
    - Automates the search for the best hyperparameters by running multiple experiments with different configurations.
    - Provides a unified interface to view and compare the results of different hyperparameter combinations.

Model Versioning:

MLflow and W&B support **model versioning**, which allows you to track different versions of a model as it progresses. This is especially useful for maintaining a history of model changes over time.

- **MLflow**: Model versioning is built-in with the mlflow.register_model() function.
- **W&B**: Automatically versions models logged through the interface, and you can track models over time in your project.

Visualizations:

Both tools offer various forms of **visualization** for metrics like accuracy, loss, and precision.

- **MLflow** provides basic visualization in its UI, including graphs for metrics and hyperparameters.
- **W&B** offers advanced visualizations, including live loss plots, accuracy curves, and even custom plots. It also supports visualizations like confusion matrices and ROC curves.

Conclusion

Experiment tracking tools like **MLflow** and **Weights & Biases** play a critical role in MLOps by providing robust mechanisms to log, visualize, and compare machine learning experiments. These tools ensure that data scientists and ML engineers can iterate on models, monitor progress, and collaborate efficiently.

- **MLflow** is ideal for users looking for an open-source, highly customizable tool to manage the full ML lifecycle.
- **W&B** offers an excellent option for teams that need more advanced visualizations, collaboration features, and seamless integration with hyperparameter optimization.

Both tools are highly valuable, and the choice depends on the specific needs of the project, such as cloud integration, real-time collaboration, or the complexity of hyperparameter tuning.

Hyperparameter Tuning and Optimization in MLOps

In machine learning, **hyperparameters** are the configuration settings or parameters that control the training process of the model. These settings are not learned from the data directly but are set manually or optimized during training. Optimizing hyperparameters is a crucial step in improving model performance, ensuring generalization, and avoiding overfitting.

In the context of **MLOps (Machine Learning Operations)**, hyperparameter tuning becomes a key activity to ensure that machine learning models deployed in production are as efficient and accurate as possible. Tuning these parameters involves using **search algorithms** and **automated processes** to find the best-performing set of hyperparameters for a given model.

Why Hyperparameter Tuning is Important in MLOps

- **Improved Model Accuracy**: Properly tuned hyperparameters can significantly improve a model's performance by ensuring that it generalizes well.
- **Optimal Resource Utilization**: Efficient hyperparameter search can help avoid wasting computational resources by finding good configurations faster.
- **Reproducibility**: In MLOps, it's crucial to document and automate the tuning process so that experiments can be reproduced and deployed reliably.

Common Hyperparameters in Machine Learning Models

- **Decision Trees / Random Forests**: max_depth, min_samples_split, min_samples_leaf, n_estimators, max_features
- **Gradient Boosting**: learning_rate, n_estimators, max_depth, subsample
- **Support Vector Machines**: C, gamma, kernel

- **Neural Networks**: learning_rate, batch_size, epochs, number of hidden layers, neurons per layer
- **K-Nearest Neighbors**: n_neighbors, weights, algorithm

Hyperparameter Tuning Techniques

1. **Grid Search**:
   - Grid search is a brute-force method that exhaustively searches through a specified set of hyperparameters.
   - It tests all possible combinations of hyperparameter values within the given ranges.
   - While it guarantees finding the best combination, it can be very computationally expensive.

Code Example (Grid Search with Scikit-Learn):

```
from sklearn.model_selection import GridSearchCV

from sklearn.ensemble import RandomForestClassifier

from sklearn.datasets import load_iris

from sklearn.model_selection import train_test_split


# Load dataset

data = load_iris()

X_train, X_test, y_train, y_test = train_test_split(data.data, data.target, test_size=0.3, random_state=42)


# Define the model

model = RandomForestClassifier()


# Set hyperparameter grid

param_grid = {
```

```
    'n_estimators': [50, 100, 200],

    'max_depth': [5, 10, None]

}


# Set up GridSearchCV

grid_search          =          GridSearchCV(estimator=model,
param_grid=param_grid, cv=5, scoring='accuracy')


# Fit grid search

grid_search.fit(X_train, y_train)


# Best parameters and score

print("Best Parameters:", grid_search.best_params_)

print("Best Score:", grid_search.best_score_)
```

2. **Random Search**:

- Random search randomly samples combinations of hyperparameters from a specified range.
- It is more efficient than grid search when the number of hyperparameters is large.
- While it doesn't guarantee finding the absolute best configuration, it often finds a good solution in less time.

Code Example (Random Search with Scikit-Learn):

```
from sklearn.model_selection import RandomizedSearchCV

from sklearn.ensemble import RandomForestClassifier

from sklearn.datasets import load_iris

from sklearn.model_selection import train_test_split
```

```python
import numpy as np

# Load dataset
data = load_iris()
X_train, X_test, y_train, y_test = train_test_split(data.data,
data.target, test_size=0.3, random_state=42)

# Define the model
model = RandomForestClassifier()

# Set hyperparameter distributions
param_dist = {
    'n_estimators': np.arange(50, 200, 50),
    'max_depth': [5, 10, None],
    'min_samples_split': [2, 5, 10]
}

# Set up RandomizedSearchCV
random_search = RandomizedSearchCV(estimator=model,
param_distributions=param_dist, n_iter=10, cv=5,
scoring='accuracy')

# Fit random search
random_search.fit(X_train, y_train)

# Best parameters and score
```

```
print("Best Parameters:", random_search.best_params_)
print("Best Score:", random_search.best_score_)
```

3. **Bayesian Optimization**:

- Bayesian optimization builds a probabilistic model of the function (hyperparameter optimization function) and uses this model to select the most promising hyperparameters.
- It is more efficient than grid search and random search because it focuses on the most promising regions of the hyperparameter space.

Tools like **Hyperopt** and **Optuna** implement Bayesian optimization for hyperparameter search.

Code Example (Bayesian Optimization with Hyperopt):

```
from hyperopt import fmin, tpe, hp, Trials

from sklearn.model_selection import train_test_split

from sklearn.ensemble import RandomForestClassifier

from sklearn.datasets import load_iris

from sklearn.metrics import accuracy_score


# Load dataset

data = load_iris()

X_train, X_test, y_train, y_test = train_test_split(data.data, data.target, test_size=0.3, random_state=42)


# Define the objective function for hyperopt

def objective(params):
```

```
model                                          =
RandomForestClassifier(n_estimators=params['n_estimators'],
max_depth=params['max_depth'])

    model.fit(X_train, y_train)

    preds = model.predict(X_test)

    accuracy = accuracy_score(y_test, preds)

    return -accuracy  # Hyperopt minimizes the objective function,
so we negate accuracy


# Define hyperparameter space

space = {

    'n_estimators': hp.choice('n_estimators', [50, 100, 200]),

    'max_depth': hp.choice('max_depth', [5, 10, None])

}


# Run the optimization

trials = Trials()

best  =  fmin(fn=objective,  space=space,  algo=tpe.suggest,
max_evals=10, trials=trials)


print("Best hyperparameters:", best)
```

1. **Genetic Algorithms**:
    o Genetic algorithms evolve hyperparameter configurations through selection, mutation, and crossover operations.
    o They can be used to search large hyperparameter spaces efficiently by combining the strengths of different configurations.

DEAP (Distributed Evolutionary Algorithms in Python) is a common library used for genetic algorithms in Python.

Automating Hyperparameter Tuning in MLOps Pipelines

Hyperparameter tuning can be integrated into an MLOps pipeline to automate the process and optimize models in production. Below are the steps to automate this process:

1. **Define the Search Space**: Use tools like **Optuna** or **Hyperopt** to define the search space for the hyperparameters.
2. **Integrate with the MLOps Platform**: Integrate the search algorithm with platforms like **MLflow**, **Kubeflow**, or **Airflow** to schedule and monitor hyperparameter optimization tasks.
3. **Track Experiments**: Use tools like **MLflow**, **Weights & Biases**, or **Comet** to track the different runs, logging hyperparameters, metrics, and models.
4. **Post-Optimization Model Deployment**: Once the best hyperparameters are found, automatically deploy the optimized model to production using MLOps tools like **Kubeflow** or **Seldon**.

Tools for Hyperparameter Tuning in MLOps

1. **Optuna**: A modern, open-source hyperparameter optimization framework that is highly efficient and integrates easily into MLOps workflows.
2. **Hyperopt**: A Python library for distributed hyperparameter optimization using the Tree-structured Parzen Estimator (TPE) algorithm.
3. **MLflow**: Supports integrating with external libraries (e.g., Hyperopt) to manage hyperparameter optimization alongside tracking and model management.

4. **Weights & Biases (W&B)**: Provides built-in support for hyperparameter sweeps, tracking hyperparameters, and comparing the performance of different configurations.
5. **Ray Tune**: A scalable hyperparameter optimization library built on top of the **Ray** distributed computing framework.

Conclusion

Hyperparameter tuning is an essential part of the MLOps pipeline, ensuring that machine learning models perform optimally. The choice of tuning technique depends on the size of the hyperparameter space, available computational resources, and time constraints. Common techniques include **Grid Search**, **Random Search**, **Bayesian Optimization**, and **Genetic Algorithms**. By automating and integrating hyperparameter tuning into an MLOps pipeline, organizations can achieve more efficient, reproducible, and scalable machine learning workflows.

Best Practices for Experiment Management in MLOps

In **MLOps**, **experiment management** refers to the process of tracking, organizing, and optimizing machine learning experiments throughout the lifecycle of model development. Managing experiments effectively is crucial for ensuring reproducibility, collaboration, and optimization in machine learning workflows. Following best practices for experiment management helps improve model performance, reduces errors, and accelerates time to deployment.

Here are the best practices for managing experiments in MLOps:

1. Version Control for Code and Data

- **Code Versioning**: Use tools like **Git** or **GitHub/GitLab** to version control your model code and ensure that all team members are working with the same version of the code.
    - Use branches for different experiments or model versions.
    - Ensure reproducibility by tagging code versions used for specific experiments.
- **Data Versioning**: Data is a critical part of machine learning experiments. Use tools like **DVC (Data Version Control)** or **LakeFS** to manage data versions and ensure consistency between datasets used across different experiments.
    - Store metadata (e.g., dataset version, transformation history) alongside your model code.

Code Example (Git Integration):

git init

git add .

git commit -m "Initial commit with model code"

git push origin main

2. Track Hyperparameters, Metrics, and Artifacts

Tracking **hyperparameters**, **metrics**, and **artifacts** is essential for understanding what led to the model's performance. Key things to track include:

- **Hyperparameters**: These control model behavior (e.g., learning_rate, n_estimators, batch_size).
- **Metrics**: Track performance metrics (e.g., accuracy, precision, recall, AUC).
- **Artifacts**: Save models, datasets, and other assets that are generated during the experiment (e.g., trained models, preprocessing pipelines).

Tools for Tracking:

- **MLflow**: Provides experiment tracking, model management, and logging.
- **Weights & Biases (W&B)**: Provides real-time visualization and logging for metrics, hyperparameters, and artifacts.
- **Comet.ml**: Tracks experiments, models, and datasets, and provides a collaborative environment.

Example Code with MLflow:

```
import mlflow

from sklearn.ensemble import RandomForestClassifier

from sklearn.datasets import load_iris

from sklearn.model_selection import train_test_split

from sklearn.metrics import accuracy_score


# Load data

data = load_iris()

X_train, X_test, y_train, y_test = train_test_split(data.data, data.target, test_size=0.3, random_state=42)


# Set up experiment

mlflow.set_experiment("Iris_Model_Experiment")


with mlflow.start_run(run_name="RandomForest_1"):

    # Log hyperparameters

    mlflow.log_param("n_estimators", 100)

    mlflow.log_param("max_depth", 10)
```

```
# Train model

model    =    RandomForestClassifier(n_estimators=100,
max_depth=10)

model.fit(X_train, y_train)


# Make predictions and log metrics

predictions = model.predict(X_test)

accuracy = accuracy_score(y_test, predictions)

mlflow.log_metric("accuracy", accuracy)


# Save model as artifact

mlflow.sklearn.log_model(model, "rf_model")
```

3. Reproducibility of Experiments

To ensure that experiments are **reproducible**, every part of the experiment (data, code, hyperparameters, environment) should be logged and versioned.

- **Random Seeds**: Set random seeds (e.g., random_state, seed) across all steps (data preprocessing, model training) to control randomness.
- **Environment Tracking**: Track the software environment (e.g., package versions) to ensure consistency across experiments. Tools like **Conda** and **Docker** can help to containerize environments.
- **Reproducibility in Distributed Systems**: Use tools like **Kubeflow** or **Airflow** to ensure that experiments in distributed systems are reproducible and scalable.

Code Example (Setting Random Seed):

```
import numpy as np

import random

import tensorflow as tf


# Set random seeds for reproducibility

np.random.seed(42)

random.seed(42)

tf.random.set_seed(42)
```

4. Collaborative Experiment Management

Machine learning projects often involve multiple team members, and collaboration is crucial for success. Make it easy for teams to share experiments, models, and results.

- Use tools like **W&B** or **MLflow** to share experiments, track changes, and provide visualizations that facilitate discussions and comparisons.
- Document the purpose of each experiment, the dataset used, and the model's performance metrics so that team members can understand the context and results.

Best Practices for Collaboration:

- **Naming Conventions**: Use consistent naming conventions for experiments, runs, and parameters to ensure clarity.
- **Sharing Results**: Share experiment results through dashboards or reports to keep stakeholders informed.

Code Example (W&B Collaboration):

```
import wandb


# Initialize W&B project
```

```
wandb.init(project="iris_classification")
```

```
# Track parameters and metrics
wandb.config.update({
    "n_estimators": 100,
    "max_depth": 10
})
```

```
# Log metrics
wandb.log({"accuracy": accuracy})
```

```
# Save model artifacts
wandb.save("model.pkl")
```

5. Automate and Optimize Experiment Workflows

Automate as much of the experiment process as possible to avoid manual errors and to scale the workflow.

- **Experiment Pipelines**: Use tools like **Kubeflow Pipelines**, **Airflow**, or **Metaflow** to automate the execution of experiments in a structured way.
- **Hyperparameter Optimization**: Automate the process of hyperparameter search with tools like **Optuna**, **Hyperopt**, or **Ray Tune**. These tools can optimize hyperparameters using search algorithms like grid search, random search, or Bayesian optimization.

Code Example (Automating with Airflow):

```
# Airflow DAG to automate the training process
from airflow import DAG
```

```
from airflow.operators.python import PythonOperator

from datetime import datetime


def train_model():

    # Insert model training code here (e.g., training a
    RandomForest)

    pass


dag = DAG('model_training', description='Train ML model',
schedule_interval='@daily', start_date=datetime(2024, 1, 1))


train_task    =    PythonOperator(task_id='train_model_task',
python_callable=train_model, dag=dag)
```

6. Track Experiment Lifecycle

Tracking the **lifecycle** of each experiment allows for better decision-making and helps monitor the evolution of the model over time.

- **State Transitions**: Track the stages of experiments (e.g., "In Progress", "Completed", "Failed") and automatically transition states as experiments progress.
- **Monitor Model Drift**: Monitor model performance over time and detect drift using **data drift** or **concept drift** detection tools.

Tools for Experiment Lifecycle Management:

- **MLflow**: Manage the entire ML lifecycle from experiment tracking to model deployment.
- **Kubeflow Pipelines**: Provides a way to automate the full pipeline and monitor the status of each experiment.

Husn Ara

7. Maintain a Centralized Experiment Repository

Maintain a central repository for storing and organizing all experiments, models, metrics, and results. This is crucial for **searchability**, ensuring that experiments are easy to compare, and making it easier to audit and track progress.

- Use **MLflow** or **Comet.ml** as a centralized experiment management tool.
- Ensure that all experiments, models, and results are logged in this central repository.

Example: Centralized Repository with MLflow

mlflow.set_experiment("central_experiment_repo")   # Centralized repo for experiments

8. Model Evaluation and Comparison

Regularly evaluate and compare different models to ensure that the best models are chosen for deployment.

- Compare models based on a consistent set of metrics (e.g., accuracy, F1 score).
- Use visualizations (e.g., confusion matrices, ROC curves) to better understand model performance.
- Store and version different models and results for future comparison.

9. Ensure Scalability of Experiment Management

As the number of experiments grows, it's important to ensure that the experiment management system can scale.

- Use **distributed training** and **cloud-based storage** to handle large datasets and computational requirements.
- Tools like **Kubeflow**, **MLflow**, and **Amazon SageMaker** provide scalable solutions for experiment tracking in cloud environments.

151

10. Document and Automate Best Practices

- **Document the Experiment Process**: Ensure that your team follows standardized procedures for tracking experiments, logging hyperparameters, and evaluating results.
- **Automate Logging**: Automate the logging process of hyperparameters, metrics, and models by integrating it into your training scripts or pipeline.

Conclusion

Effective **experiment management** is at the core of successful **MLOps** implementations. It ensures that machine learning workflows are reproducible, scalable, and optimized for performance. By following these best practices—such as versioning code and data, tracking hyperparameters and metrics, automating workflows, and fostering collaboration—you can build a robust experiment management system that drives the success of your machine learning projects.

Chapter-7 Model Packaging and Deployment

Introduction to Model Packaging

Model packaging is the process of preparing a trained machine learning (ML) model for deployment by bundling the model along with its dependencies and configurations into a portable and reusable format. In MLOps (Machine Learning Operations), model packaging ensures that models are easily transferable across different environments, such as from development to production, while maintaining consistency and scalability.

Why Model Packaging is Important in MLOps

1. **Reproducibility**: Packaging models ensures that the same model, with its specific dependencies, can be run anywhere without environment inconsistencies.
2. **Deployment Efficiency**: It simplifies the process of deploying models across multiple platforms or cloud services, ensuring faster delivery to production.

3. **Portability**: Models can be easily moved between different environments (development, testing, and production) without needing to manually replicate the setup.
4. **Dependency Management**: Ensures that the model's dependencies (libraries, packages, configurations) are included, so no critical component is missing at the time of deployment.
5. **Scalability**: Packaging helps when scaling models across distributed systems or different cloud infrastructures.

Key Components of Model Packaging

1. **Model Artifact**: The saved and serialized machine learning model (e.g., .pkl, .joblib, .h5 files). It contains the learned parameters and structure of the model.
2. **Dependencies**: The libraries and packages required to run the model. These include machine learning frameworks like TensorFlow, PyTorch, or Scikit-learn, and other utility libraries.
3. **Environment Specification**: Documentation of the environment in which the model was trained, usually provided via:
   o requirements.txt for Python packages.
   o Dockerfile for complete containerized environments.
   o Conda environment (environment.yml).
4. **Configuration Files**: Configuration files store specific details like hyperparameters, input data formats, and any additional settings needed to run the model in different environments.
5. **Inference Scripts**: Scripts that handle how the model will make predictions in production, including pre-processing of input data and post-processing of predictions.

Model Packaging Tools

1. **Docker**: A popular tool that allows for complete environment packaging. It containers the model along with its dependencies, OS-level libraries, and runtime

environment to ensure consistency across different platforms.

2. **TensorFlow Serving**: A specific solution for deploying TensorFlow models that provides high-performance serving of ML models in production environments.
3. **ONNX (Open Neural Network Exchange)**: ONNX provides an open-source format for representing machine learning models, making it easier to port models between different frameworks and tools.
4. **MLflow Models**: MLflow supports packaging models for multiple platforms, including Docker and cloud services like AWS SageMaker and Google AI Platform.

Model Packaging Workflow

1. **Model Serialization**: Save the trained model into a specific format (e.g., .joblib for Scikit-learn, .h5 for TensorFlow).
2. **Environment Specification**: List all the dependencies required by the model, either using requirements.txt, a Conda environment file, or a Dockerfile.
3. **Containerization (optional)**: For reproducibility across various platforms, use Docker to create an image that contains the model, its environment, and inference scripts.
4. **Test the Package**: Before deploying, test the packaged model in a staging or testing environment to ensure it works as expected.
5. **Deploy the Model**: Use tools like Kubernetes, Docker Swarm, or cloud services to deploy the packaged model into production.

Challenges in Model Packaging

- **Dependency Conflicts**: Ensuring that all the libraries required for the model are compatible and work across different environments.
- **Security**: Ensuring the packaged model is secure, particularly if sensitive data was used in training the model.
- **Optimization**: Keeping the size of the package minimal while ensuring all required dependencies are included,

especially when deploying to resource-constrained environments like edge devices.

Model packaging is a crucial step in ensuring that machine learning models can be easily deployed, scaled, and maintained in production environments. In MLOps, efficient packaging ensures that the entire machine learning lifecycle, from development to deployment, is smooth, consistent, and automated.

Dockerizing Machine Learning Models

Dockerizing a machine learning model involves creating a Docker container that packages your ML model, along with its dependencies, into a portable environment. This ensures that the model can run consistently across different machines and environments, which is critical for deployment in production.

Below is a step-by-step guide with code on how to dockerize a machine learning model.

Steps for Dockerizing a Machine Learning Model

1. Set Up Your Model

Train your model and save it to disk. Below is an example where we use Scikit-learn to train a simple model, serialize it, and save it as a file.

```
# train_model.py

import joblib

from sklearn.datasets import load_iris
```

```
from sklearn.ensemble import RandomForestClassifier

# Load dataset

iris = load_iris()

X, y = iris.data, iris.target

# Train a model

model = RandomForestClassifier()

model.fit(X, y)

# Save the model to disk

joblib.dump(model, 'model.pkl')
```

2. Create an Inference Script

Once your model is trained, create an inference script to load the model and make predictions based on new input data.

```
# inference.py

import joblib

from flask import Flask, request, jsonify

# Load the model
```

```python
model = joblib.load('model.pkl')


app = Flask(__name__)


@app.route('/predict', methods=['POST'])

def predict():

    data = request.get_json()

    prediction = model.predict([data['features']])

    return jsonify({'prediction': prediction.tolist()})


if __name__ == '__main__':

app.run(host='0.0.0.0', port=5000)
```

This script uses Flask to serve the model and provides an API endpoint for predictions.

3. **Create a Dockerfile**

The Dockerfile defines the environment in which the model will run. It installs the necessary libraries, copies the model and scripts, and runs the Flask server.

```
# Use an official Python runtime as a parent image

FROM python:3.8-slim
```

```
# Set the working directory in the container

WORKDIR /app


# Copy the current directory contents into the container at /app

COPY . /app


# Install any needed packages specified in requirements.txt

RUN pip install --no-cache-dir -r requirements.txt


# Make port 5000 available to the world outside this container

EXPOSE 5000


# Define environment variable

ENV NAME World


# Run the application

CMD ["python", "inference.py"]
```

4. **Create a** requirements.txt **File**

List all the Python dependencies needed for your model to run.

```
Flask==2.0.3
```

scikit-learn==1.0.1

joblib==1.1.0

5. **Build the Docker Image**

Once the Dockerfile and necessary files are ready, build the Docker image using the Docker CLI.

Build the image

docker build -t ml-model .

6. **Run the Docker Container**

Run the Docker container that will serve your machine learning model.

Run the container

docker run -p 5000:5000 ml-model

This will start a Flask server inside the container, exposing port 5000 for making predictions.

7. **Test the Model API**

You can test the model by sending a POST request with data to the /predict endpoint.

Send a request to the model's API

curl -X POST -H "Content-Type: application/json" \

-d '{"features": [5.1, 3.5, 1.4, 0.2]}' \

http://localhost:5000/predict

Benefits of Dockerizing Machine Learning Models

- **Portability**: The model can be deployed consistently across various environments (local machine, cloud, or on-premise).
- **Reproducibility**: Ensures that the environment is identical across all stages—development, testing, and production.
- **Isolation**: Models run in isolated containers, ensuring no conflict with other models or applications running on the same machine.
- **Scalability**: Docker makes it easier to scale models by orchestrating multiple containers across different environments.

Advanced: Using Docker Compose for Multi-Container Applications

If your application consists of multiple services (e.g., model server, database, etc.), you can use Docker Compose to manage multi-container setups.

```
# docker-compose.yml

version: '3'


services:

  ml-model:

    build: .

    ports:

      - "5000:5000"
```

Run the application with docker-compose:

docker-compose up

This allows you to scale and orchestrate multiple services easily.

Dockerizing machine learning models is a powerful way to ensure smooth deployment, scalability, and management of models across various platforms. The Dockerfile, along with the necessary dependencies and configurations, ensures that the model runs consistently, making it a vital part of MLOps practices.

Deploying Models with Kubernetes and Helm

Kubernetes (K8s) and Helm are widely used tools for deploying and managing machine learning models at scale. Kubernetes provides a robust platform for container orchestration, ensuring that ML models can be deployed, scaled, and maintained efficiently across distributed environments. Helm, often called the "package manager for Kubernetes," simplifies the deployment process by allowing you to define, install, and upgrade Kubernetes applications using "charts."

Here's a detailed guide on how to deploy machine learning models with Kubernetes and Helm.

Why Use Kubernetes and Helm for ML Model Deployment?

1. **Scalability**: Kubernetes allows you to easily scale your model deployment based on load and resource requirements.
2. **Load Balancing**: Kubernetes can distribute incoming traffic to multiple replicas of your model, ensuring better performance and high availability.
3. **Auto-healing**: If a model deployment fails or crashes, Kubernetes can automatically restart or reschedule the pod.

4. **Versioning and Rollback**: Helm provides version control for deployments, making it easy to roll back to a previous stable version if needed.

Steps for Deploying ML Models with Kubernetes and Helm

1. Containerize the Machine Learning Model

Before deploying the model, it needs to be containerized (using Docker). Refer to the section on Dockerizing a Machine Learning model.

2. Set Up Kubernetes Cluster

If you don't already have a Kubernetes cluster, you can set up a local one using minikube for development or use a managed Kubernetes service like Google Kubernetes Engine (GKE), Amazon Elastic Kubernetes Service (EKS), or Azure Kubernetes Service (AKS) for production.

To start with Minikube:

minikube start

3. Write Kubernetes Deployment and Service YAML Files

The deployment file defines how the containerized model will be deployed on Kubernetes, including replicas, resources, and the image to use. The service file exposes the deployment to the outside world.

Here is an example Kubernetes deployment and service for your model:

Deployment YAML (deployment.yaml)

```yaml
apiVersion: apps/v1

kind: Deployment

metadata:

  name: ml-model-deployment

spec:

  replicas: 3

  selector:

    matchLabels:

      app: ml-model

  template:

    metadata:

      labels:

        app: ml-model

    spec:

      containers:

      - name: ml-model-container

        image: ml-model:latest  # Replace with your image

        ports:

        - containerPort: 5000
```

Service YAML (service.yaml)

```
apiVersion: v1

kind: Service

metadata:

  name: ml-model-service

spec:

  selector:

    app: ml-model

  ports:

    - protocol: TCP

    port: 80

targetPort: 5000

  type: LoadBalancer
```

These files define:

- **Deployment**: It runs three replicas of the containerized model.
- **Service**: It exposes the model to the outside using a load balancer.

4. Deploy to Kubernetes

After setting up the configuration files, you can deploy them using kubectl.

```
# Apply the deployment

kubectl apply -f deployment.yaml
```

```
# Apply the service
```

```
kubectl apply -f service.yaml
```

Check the status of your deployment:

```
kubectl get pods
```

Get the external IP of the service to access the model:

```
kubectl get svc
```

5. **Using Helm for Model Deployment**

Helm simplifies Kubernetes deployment by packaging all the YAML files and configuration into charts, making it easier to manage complex deployments.

Creating a Helm Chart for the ML Model

```
helm create ml-model-chart
```

This will generate a default directory structure for the chart:

```
ml-model-chart/

  charts/

  templates/

deployment.yaml

service.yaml

values.yaml

Chart.yaml
```

Edit the deployment.yaml and **service.yaml** in the templates/ folder, similar to the YAML files created earlier, but with Helm templating variables:

Helm Deployment YAML (templates/deployment.yaml)

apiVersion: apps/v1

kind: Deployment

metadata:

  name: {{ .Release.Name }}-ml-model-deployment

spec:

  replicas: {{ .Values.replicaCount }}

  selector:

matchLabels:

   app: {{ .Release.Name }}

  template:

   metadata:

   labels:

    app: {{ .Release.Name }}

  spec:

  containers:

  - name: ml-model-container

   image: {{ .Values.image.repository }}:{{ .Values.image.tag }}

```
ports:

- containerPort: 5000
```

Helm Values File (values.yaml)

```
replicaCount: 3


image:

  repository: ml-model

  tag: latest


service:

  type: LoadBalancer

  port: 80
```

Install the Helm Chart

After creating the chart, you can install it into the Kubernetes cluster:

```
helm install ml-model ./ml-model-chart
```

This deploys your model and service using the configurations defined in the chart.

Updating the Helm Chart

If you need to update the model (e.g., new model version or replica count), modify the values.yaml and use Helm to upgrade the deployment:

helm upgrade ml-model ./ml-model-chart

Rollback with Helm

If something goes wrong during the update, you can easily roll back to a previous version:

helm rollback ml-model 1

Monitoring and Managing the Deployment

Once deployed, you can monitor and manage the Kubernetes deployment using various tools like Prometheus, Grafana, and Kubernetes dashboards.

Prometheus and Grafana provide robust metrics collection and visualization, allowing you to monitor model performance, container resource usage, and more.

Benefits of Using Kubernetes and Helm for ML Models

- **Scalability**: Easily scale model replicas to handle increased load.
- **High Availability**: Kubernetes ensures model availability by auto-healing crashed pods.
- **Version Control and Rollbacks**: Helm allows easy version control of deployments, enabling smooth upgrades and rollbacks.
- **Efficient Resource Utilization**: Kubernetes manages container resources efficiently, optimizing CPU and memory usage.

Conclusion

Deploying machine learning models with Kubernetes and Helm allows for a robust, scalable, and easily manageable solution. With Kubernetes, you can scale, monitor, and manage your deployments in production efficiently, while Helm simplifies versioning, upgrades, and rollback of deployments, making it ideal for managing large-scale machine learning operations.

Model Serving with Flask, FastAPI, and TensorFlow Serving

In the machine learning lifecycle, model serving is a crucial step where trained models are made available for use in real-time applications. There are several frameworks and tools to serve machine learning models, each with its unique advantages. Here, we will cover how to serve models using Flask, FastAPI, and TensorFlow Serving.

1. Model Serving with Flask

Flask is a lightweight Python web framework commonly used to deploy machine learning models in real-time applications. Here's how you can serve a machine learning model using Flask.

Steps to Serve a Model with Flask:

1. **Train and Save the Model** Before serving the model, you need a trained machine learning model saved using a library like pickle or joblib.

import pickle

Train a simple model (e.g., sklearn)

from sklearn.datasets import load_iris

from sklearn.ensemble import RandomForestClassifier

Load dataset and train the model

```python
iris = load_iris()

model = RandomForestClassifier()

model.fit(iris.data, iris.target)


# Save the model

with open("model.pkl", "wb") as model_file:

pickle.dump(model, model_file)
```

2. **Create Flask App** Set up a Flask web server to load and serve the trained model.

```python
from flask import Flask, request, jsonify

import pickle


# Load the saved model

with open("model.pkl", "rb") as model_file:

    model = pickle.load(model_file)


# Initialize Flask app

app = Flask(__name__)


@app.route('/predict', methods=['POST'])
```

```
def predict():

    data = request.get_json()

    prediction = model.predict([data['input']])

    return jsonify({'prediction': int(prediction[0])})



if __name__ == "__main__":

app.run(debug=True)
```

3. **Run the Flask Server** Run the app with:

```
python app.py
```

1. The server will listen for incoming POST requests at the /predict endpoint and return predictions based on the input data.

2. Model Serving with FastAPI

FastAPI is a modern web framework for building APIs with Python. It is faster than Flask, supports asynchronous requests, and provides automatic documentation through OpenAPI and Swagger.

Steps to Serve a Model with FastAPI:

1. **Install FastAPI and Uvicorn**

   Install the required libraries:

```
pip install fastapiuvicorn
```

2. **Create FastAPI App**

Here's an example of serving a model using FastAPI:

```
from fastapi import FastAPI

from pydantic import BaseModel

import pickle


# Load the saved model

with open("model.pkl", "rb") as model_file:

    model = pickle.load(model_file)


# Initialize FastAPI app

app = FastAPI()


# Define request body structure

class InputData(BaseModel):

    input: list


@app.post('/predict')

async def predict(data: InputData):

    prediction = model.predict([data.input])

    return {'prediction': int(prediction[0])}
```

```
if __name__ == "__main__":
```

```
import uvicorn
```

```
uvicorn.run(app, host="0.0.0.0", port=8000)
```

Run the FastAPI Server

Use uvicorn to run the FastAPI app:

```
uvicornapp:app–reload
```

1. FastAPI will serve the model at http://localhost:8000/predict, handling requests in an efficient and asynchronous manner.

3. Model Serving with TensorFlow Serving

TensorFlow Serving is a high-performance system specifically designed to serve machine learning models, especially TensorFlow models, in production environments. It can handle multiple models and versions, making it ideal for complex ML workflows.

Steps to Serve a Model with TensorFlow Serving:

1. **Save a TensorFlow Model**

   To serve a model with TensorFlow Serving, save it in TensorFlow's SavedModel format.

```
import tensorflow as tf
```

```
# Create and train a simple model
```

```
mnist = tf.keras.datasets.mnist

(x_train, y_train), (x_test, y_test) = mnist.load_data()

model = tf.keras.Sequential([

tf.keras.layers.Flatten(input_shape=(28, 28)),

tf.keras.layers.Dense(128, activation='relu'),

tf.keras.layers.Dropout(0.2),

tf.keras.layers.Dense(10)

])

model.compile(optimizer='adam',

loss=tf.keras.losses.SparseCategoricalCrossentropy(from_logits
=True),

        metrics=['accuracy'])
model.fit(x_train, y_train, epochs=5)



# Save the model

model.save('models/mnist/1/')   # Save model in TensorFlow's
SavedModel format
```

2. Install TensorFlow Serving

Install TensorFlow Serving using Docker:

```
docker pull tensorflow/serving
```

3. **Run TensorFlow Serving**

Run TensorFlow Serving with the saved model:

docker run -p 8501:8501 --name=tf_serving_mnist \

  --mount type=bind,source=$(pwd)/models/mnist,target=/models/mnist \

  -e MODEL_NAME=mnist -t tensorflow/serving

4. Make Predictions Using TensorFlow Serving

You can send a POST request to TensorFlow Serving to get predictions:

curl -d '{"signature_name":"serving_default","instances":[[0.0, ...]]}' \

-X POST http://localhost:8501/v1/models/mnist:predict

1. TensorFlow Serving provides a robust and scalable way to serve TensorFlow models in production, handling large-scale deployments.

Conclusion

Whether you're using Flask, FastAPI, or TensorFlow Serving, model serving is a critical component of any machine learning pipeline. Flask and FastAPI are suitable for smaller projects or real-time applications where Python is the dominant stack. TensorFlow Serving is ideal for larger-scale, production-level deployments, particularly when managing TensorFlow models. By selecting the right serving framework based on your use case, you can ensure scalability, performance, and efficiency in delivering machine learning predictions.

Chapter-8 Continuous Integration & Continuous Deployment (CI/CD) for ML

CI/CD Workflows in MLOps

CI/CD Workflows in MLOps

Continuous Integration and Continuous Deployment (CI/CD) are essential processes in MLOps (Machine Learning Operations), automating the lifecycle of machine learning (ML) models. By setting up CI/CD workflows, teams can deploy and update models quickly, ensure reproducibility, and improve the efficiency and quality of ML products in production.

1. Continuous Integration (CI) for ML

In the context of machine learning, Continuous Integration focuses on ensuring that code, data, and model components are consistently tested, integrated, and validated throughout the ML pipeline.

Key Components of CI in MLOps:

1. **Code Versioning**: Use version control (e.g., Git) to track code changes and maintain a reliable history of different stages in the ML lifecycle.
2. **Data Validation**: Track data versions and ensure data quality. This is crucial since ML models depend heavily on data, and changes in data distribution can impact model accuracy.
3. **Automated Testing**: Testing in CI for ML goes beyond unit and integration tests:
    o **Data Tests**: Ensure data consistency and integrity (e.g., no missing values, correct formats).
    o **Model Tests**: Ensure model functionality with tests such as smoke testing (e.g., making predictions on sample data) and unit tests for model methods.
4. **Model Validation**: Automated validation ensures that the model meets a set of predefined quality benchmarks. This may involve checking the model's accuracy, F1 score, or other metrics based on the model's purpose.

Example CI Workflow for MLOps:

Example CI Configuration using GitHub Actions

name: ML CI Pipeline

on:

 push:

  branches:

   - main

jobs:

 build-and-test:

  runs-on: ubuntu-latest

```
steps:
  - name: Checkout Code
    uses: actions/checkout@v2

  - name: Set up Python
    uses: actions/setup-python@v2
    with:
      python-version: '3.8'

  - name: Install Dependencies
    run: |
      pip install -r requirements.txt
      pip install -r test_requirements.txt

  - name: Run Data and Model Tests
    run: pytest tests/
```

2. Continuous Deployment (CD) for ML

Continuous Deployment focuses on automating the release process, enabling fast, efficient, and safe deployment of ML models into production.

Key Components of CD in MLOps:

1. **Model Packaging**: Package the ML model into a portable format (e.g., Docker containers or SavedModel for TensorFlow). This ensures that models can be easily deployed across different environments.

2. **Model Registry**: Register models to track versions and metadata, ensuring each model's lineage and facilitating rollback if needed.
3. **Automated Model Deployment**: Automatically deploy models using orchestration tools like Kubernetes, Jenkins, or ML-specific tools (e.g., Kubeflow, Seldon Core). Deployment can happen on different environments, from staging to production.
4. **Monitoring and Feedback Loops**: Monitor models in production for drift and performance degradation. Set up automated retraining or alerts if significant performance changes are detected.

Example CD Workflow for MLOps:

Example CD Configuration using GitHub Actions with Docker

name: ML CD Pipeline

on:

  push:

    branches:

      - main

jobs:

  deploy:

    runs-on: ubuntu-latest

    steps:

      - name: Checkout Code

        uses: actions/checkout@v2

      - name: Set up Docker Buildx

```
uses: docker/setup-buildx-action@v1

  - name: Login to Docker Hub
    uses: docker/login-action@v1
    with:
      username: ${{ secrets.DOCKER_USERNAME }}
      password: ${{ secrets.DOCKER_PASSWORD }}

  - name: Build and Push Docker Image
    run: |
      docker build -t username/ml-model:latest .
      docker push username/ml-model:latest

  - name: Deploy to Kubernetes
    run: |
kubectl apply -f deployment.yaml
```

Benefits of CI/CD in MLOps

- **Automation**: Reduces the need for manual intervention, speeding up the model development and deployment lifecycle.
- **Quality Control**: Ensures consistency and reliability with each change, reducing bugs or performance issues in production.
- **Scalability**: Allows data scientists and ML engineers to quickly adapt to data changes, model updates, and deployment requirements.
- **Reproducibility**: Ensures that model versions, training environments, and data are tracked and reproducible.

By implementing CI/CD workflows in MLOps, organizations can keep their ML models robust and up-to-date, while minimizing errors and optimizing time-to-production for new ML features and models.

Automated Testing of ML Models

Automated testing is a critical part of the Machine Learning (ML) lifecycle, enabling teams to ensure that models function as expected, provide consistent results, and meet quality standards throughout the pipeline. In MLOps, automated testing is integrated into Continuous Integration (CI) and Continuous Deployment (CD) workflows, focusing on verifying data, model performance, and the integrity of ML workflows. This process reduces errors and manual intervention, promoting reliable and reproducible model deployment.

Types of Automated Testing in MLOps

Automated testing in ML consists of various testing layers designed to cover different aspects of data and model integrity:

1. **Data Validation**: Validates data quality, consistency, and correctness.
2. **Unit Testing**: Tests individual model components (e.g., functions and classes) for correct behavior.
3. **Model Validation Testing**: Tests the overall model performance on training and testing datasets.
4. **Integration Testing**: Ensures the integration of multiple components, such as data pipelines and model outputs, function as expected.
5. **End-to-End Testing**: Validates the entire ML pipeline, from data ingestion to model prediction.
6. **Regression Testing**: Ensures new changes don't negatively impact existing model performance.

Code Examples for Automated Testing

Below are examples of how you might set up automated testing for ML models using Python, pytest, and the unittest library.

1. Data Validation with Great Expectations

Using Great Expectations for data validation, we can enforce data schema constraints, detect missing values, and monitor for anomalies.

```python
import great_expectations as ge


# Sample dataset
data = {
    "age": [25, 30, 45, None, 27],
    "income": [50000, 60000, 55000, 45000, None]
}
df = ge.from_pandas(pd.DataFrame(data))


# Expectations
df.expect_column_values_to_be_of_type("age", "int")
df.expect_column_values_to_not_be_null("age")
df.expect_column_values_to_be_between("income",
min_value=40000, max_value=70000)
```

2. Unit Testing for ML Model Functions

The following example demonstrates unit tests for individual functions in the model, like preprocessing and prediction methods.

```python
import unittest

import numpy as np

from my_ml_pipeline import preprocess_data, predict


class TestMLFunctions(unittest.TestCase):
    def test_preprocess_data(self):
        sample_data = np.array([[25, 60000]])
        processed_data = preprocess_data(sample_data)
        self.assertEqual(processed_data.shape, (1, 2))


    def test_predict(self):
        sample_input = np.array([[0.5, 1.5]])
        prediction = predict(sample_input)
        self.assertIn(prediction, [0, 1])  # binary classifier example


if __name__ == '__main__':
    unittest.main()
```

3. Model Performance Validation with Pytest

Using pytest, we can automate performance metrics validation to ensure the model meets required accuracy and precision thresholds.

```python
import pytest

from sklearn.metrics import accuracy_score

from my_ml_pipeline import load_data, train_model, get_test_set
```

```
@pytest.fixture

def model():

train_data, _ = load_data()

   model = train_model(train_data)

   return model


def test_model_accuracy(model):

   _, test_data = get_test_set()

X_test, y_test = test_data

y_pred = model.predict(X_test)

   accuracy = accuracy_score(y_test, y_pred)

   assert accuracy >= 0.8, "Model accuracy below acceptable
threshold"
```

4. Integration Testing with Data Pipeline and Model Prediction

Integration testing checks that the data preprocessing pipeline and model predictions work as expected.

```
import unittest

from my_pipeline import data_pipeline, model


class TestPipelineIntegration(unittest.TestCase):

   def test_pipeline_integration(self):

sample_data = {"age": 29, "income": 45000}

processed_data = data_pipeline.process(sample_data)

      prediction = model.predict(processed_data)
```

```
self.assertIn(prediction, [0, 1])  # Binary classification output


if __name__ == "__main__":

unittest.main()
```

5. Regression Testing for Model Drift Detection

With pytest and previous metrics, we can validate that the model performance has not regressed compared to previous baselines.

```
import pytest

from sklearn.metrics import f1_score

from my_ml_pipeline import load_latest_model, get_test_set


# Previous F1 score benchmark for model regression testing

PREVIOUS_F1_SCORE = 0.85


def test_model_regression():

    model = load_latest_model()

    _, test_data = get_test_set()

X_test, y_test = test_data

y_pred = model.predict(X_test)

    f1 = f1_score(y_test, y_pred)

    assert f1 >= PREVIOUS_F1_SCORE, "Model F1 score has
regressed below previous benchmark"
```

Best Practices in Automated Testing for ML Models

1. **Maintain Baselines**: Regularly update baseline metrics for model quality to detect performance degradation over time.
2. **Modular Tests**: Separate tests for data validation, model component tests, and integration tests to isolate issues quickly.
3. **Automate and Integrate**: Use CI/CD tools to integrate automated testing into the deployment pipeline, such as Jenkins, GitHub Actions, or CircleCI.
4. **Data Drift and Model Monitoring**: Automate monitoring for data drift and changes in model performance after deployment.

Conclusion

Automated testing of ML models helps ensure reliability and maintainability across the entire ML lifecycle. By combining data validation, unit tests, integration tests, and performance checks, MLOps teams can confidently deploy models, prevent regressions, and quickly detect issues. Integrating these tests into a CI/CD pipeline provides continuous validation for each model change, making it a key practice in robust and scalable machine learning systems.

Building and Deploying ML Pipelines

In Machine Learning Operations (MLOps), ML pipelines enable teams to automate the end-to-end machine learning workflow, from data ingestion to model training, validation, deployment, and monitoring. They streamline the repetitive tasks involved in model building and ensure consistent results, supporting scalability and reliability across multiple stages of model development and deployment.

Key Stages in ML Pipelines

1. **Data Ingestion and Preprocessing**:
   - Involves collecting raw data from various sources (databases, APIs, files) and preparing it for analysis by cleaning, normalizing, and transforming the data.
   - Data pipelines may include transformations like handling missing values, encoding categorical variables, scaling, and normalizing features to make data suitable for model training.
2. **Feature Engineering**:
   - This stage involves creating new features or modifying existing ones to improve model accuracy.
   - Techniques include feature selection, extraction, and transformation.
3. **Model Training and Validation**:
   - The model is trained using labeled data, followed by testing and validation on unseen data to evaluate performance.
   - Automated training pipelines can handle hyperparameter tuning using grid search or randomized search, allowing optimization for model accuracy.
4. **Model Evaluation**:
   - Ensures the model meets specified performance criteria on key metrics like accuracy, precision, recall, F1-score, or custom business metrics.
   - Performance tracking tools (e.g., MLflow, Weights & Biases) can log results, keeping track of experiment history and benchmarking.
5. **Model Packaging**:
   - The trained model, along with dependencies and configurations, is packaged into a deployable format, commonly using Docker for containerization.
   - Dockerized models are easier to deploy consistently across different environments, ensuring compatibility and reliability.
6. **Model Deployment**:
   - Deploying the model for real-time or batch predictions on a scalable platform, often using

Kubernetes, cloud services, or serverless functions.

- A/B testing and shadow testing can be used during deployment to assess performance without affecting production.

7. **Monitoring and Maintenance**:

- Continuous monitoring of deployed models is critical to detect data drift, concept drift, or performance degradation.
- Tools like Grafana or Prometheus can be integrated to trigger alerts and allow retraining if the model's accuracy drops below a certain threshold.

Code Example for Building a Simple ML Pipeline Using Kubeflow

Below is a simple example using Kubeflow Pipelines, a tool that allows orchestrating machine learning workflows on Kubernetes.

```
from kfp import dsl

import kfp.compiler as compiler


# Define pipeline components

@dsl.component

def load_data_op():

    # Load and prepare data code here

    pass


@dsl.component

def preprocess_data_op(data):

    # Preprocess data

    pass
```

```python
@dsl.component
def train_model_op(processed_data):
    # Model training code
    pass


@dsl.component
def evaluate_model_op(model):
    # Model evaluation code
    pass


# Define pipeline workflow
@dsl.pipeline(
    name="Simple ML Pipeline",
    description="An example ML pipeline"
)
def simple_ml_pipeline():
    data = load_data_op()
processed_data = preprocess_data_op(data)
    model = train_model_op(processed_data)
evaluate_model_op(model)


# Compile and run pipeline
if __name__ == "__main__":
```

```
compiler.Compiler().compile(simple_ml_pipeline,
'simple_ml_pipeline.yaml')
```

Deployment with CI/CD Integration

To deploy an ML pipeline effectively, MLOps engineers use CI/CD tools like Jenkins, GitLab CI, or GitHub Actions. These tools help automate tasks such as building Docker images, running unit tests, and deploying models to production environments.

Best Practices in ML Pipeline Development

1. **Modularity**: Design modular pipeline components to facilitate easier debugging, maintenance, and testing.
2. **Logging and Monitoring**: Track pipeline steps, log outputs, and monitor performance to quickly detect issues.
3. **Versioning**: Use version control for both code and data to reproduce models accurately and audit changes.
4. **Automated Retraining**: Implement triggers based on model performance and data drift for automatic retraining.

Conclusion

Building and deploying ML pipelines effectively automates the ML workflow, enabling scalable, efficient, and consistent delivery of ML models to production. Leveraging modern tools like Kubeflow, Docker, and CI/CD frameworks, teams can ensure reliable deployments and continuous improvements to keep ML models in alignment with business goals.

Integrating Jenkins and GitLab for ML CI/CD

Integrating Jenkins and GitLab provides a robust Continuous Integration and Continuous Deployment (CI/CD) pipeline for machine learning (ML) projects. This setup leverages GitLab's repository and version control capabilities alongside Jenkins' automation and orchestration strengths, streamlining the process of building, testing, and deploying ML models.

Why Integrate Jenkins and GitLab?

1. **Enhanced Automation**: Jenkins automates workflows that GitLab initiates, such as testing code updates or retraining ML models.
2. **Version Control**: GitLab offers seamless version control, tracking changes in model code, data, and configuration.
3. **Continuous Deployment**: With Jenkins managing CI/CD tasks, ML models can be automatically deployed to production environments, reducing manual interventions and deployment times.
4. **Efficient Collaboration**: GitLab's integrated environment for repositories, issues, and merge requests allows teams to collaborate efficiently on ML workflows.

Setting Up Jenkins and GitLab for ML CI/CD

1. **Connect GitLab with Jenkins**:
   o Go to GitLab, navigate to **Settings > Integrations**, and set up a **WebHook** pointing to Jenkins. This allows GitLab to notify Jenkins about repository events, like code commits.
   o Configure Jenkins to listen for push events from GitLab using a plugin, such as **GitLab Plugin** or **GitLab Hook Plugin**.
2. **Create a Jenkins Pipeline Job**:

- o In Jenkins, create a new **Pipeline Job** and set it up to fetch the code from the GitLab repository.
- o Specify the repository URL and credentials. Use GitLab's personal access tokens for secure access.

3. **Define the ML Pipeline in Jenkins**:
   - o Create a Jenkinsfile in the root of your GitLab repository to define your pipeline stages:
     - **Data Preprocessing**: Process and clean raw data.
     - **Model Training**: Train the ML model using the latest data.
     - **Model Validation**: Validate model performance on a test set.
     - **Deployment**: Deploy the model if validation metrics are satisfactory.

Example Jenkinsfile:

```
pipeline {

  agent any


  environment {

    REPO_URL      =      'https://gitlab.com/username/project-name.git'
  }


  stages {
stage('Clone Repository') {

      steps {

        git url: "${REPO_URL}", branch: 'main'

      }

    }
```

```
stage('Install Dependencies') {
        steps {
sh 'pip install -r requirements.txt'
        }
    }


stage('Data Preprocessing') {
        steps {
sh 'python scripts/preprocess_data.py'
        }
    }


stage('Model Training') {
        steps {
sh 'python scripts/train_model.py'
        }
    }


stage('Model Validation') {
        steps {
sh 'python scripts/validate_model.py'
        }
    }
```

```
stage('Deploy Model') {

      when {

        expression { returncurrentBuild.result == 'SUCCESS' }

      }

      steps {

        echo 'Deploying model...'
sh 'python scripts/deploy_model.py'

      }

    }

  }

}
```

4. **Set Up GitLab CI/CD for Merge Request Validation**:
   o Use GitLab CI/CD for initial testing to validate merge requests and code changes before Jenkins deploys the model. In .gitlab-ci.yml, configure tests for code quality, unit tests, and data integrity checks.

Example GitLab .gitlab-ci.yml:

```
stages:

  - test


test_code:

  stage: test

  script:

    - python -m unittest discover tests/

    - flake8 .
```

Testing and Deployment Automation

1. **Automated Testing**:
   - o Configure unit tests and validation scripts in both Jenkins and GitLab. Jenkins can trigger model performance tests, such as A/B testing or shadow deployment.
2. **Deployment Automation**:
   - o Use Jenkins to automate the deployment of the trained model to production. Docker containers and Kubernetes can streamline this by making the model portable and scalable.

Best Practices for Integrating Jenkins and GitLab for ML CI/CD

1. **Model Versioning**:
   - o Use GitLab's tagging and branching to keep track of different model versions and configurations.
2. **Environment Isolation**:
   - o Use Docker to isolate environments and ensure consistency across development, testing, and production stages.
3. **Rollback Strategies**:
   - o Implement rollback policies in Jenkins to restore previous model versions if the deployed model fails.
4. **Secure Access**:
   - o Use API tokens and restrict permissions between GitLab and Jenkins to maintain security.

Conclusion

Integrating Jenkins with GitLab for ML CI/CD creates a powerful, automated pipeline that accelerates model deployment and monitoring while reducing human error. This setup enables data science teams to confidently deliver reliable, up-to-date models into production, optimizing for performance and scalability in dynamic ML environments.

Chapter-9 Monitoring and Logging in MLOps

Importance of Monitoring Deployed Models

Monitoring deployed machine learning (ML) models is critical for ensuring that they continue to deliver reliable, accurate, and fair predictions. Once a model is in production, it is exposed to real-world data, which may differ significantly from the training data. By implementing monitoring, data science teams can identify and address issues as they arise, maintain model performance, and uphold trust in the system. Here are some key reasons monitoring is essential:

1. **Detecting Data Drift**:
   o Over time, the data a model encounters in production may shift, causing data drift—a change in the distribution of input data. This can affect model accuracy and degrade performance.
   o Monitoring for data drift helps teams catch shifts early, enabling retraining with updated data to maintain model relevance.
2. **Managing Concept Drift**:
   o Concept drift occurs when the underlying relationship between input features and the

target variable changes over time. For instance, customer behavior may evolve, rendering a sales prediction model less accurate.

- o Monitoring metrics like prediction error rates can detect concept drift, allowing for model adjustments or retraining to adapt to new patterns.

3. **Performance Degradation**:
   - o As models interact with real-world environments, changes in data quality, sampling, or unforeseen events may impact their predictive accuracy.
   - o Regularly assessing performance metrics, such as accuracy, precision, recall, and F1 score, allows for timely interventions to prevent erroneous predictions.

4. **Fairness and Bias Detection**:
   - o Models may become biased if the input data starts representing one group over others or if changes in the system favor certain demographics unintentionally.
   - o Monitoring fairness metrics, such as demographic parity or equal opportunity, ensures that the model continues to serve all groups equitably, avoiding ethical and legal risks.

5. **Compliance and Regulatory Requirements**:
   - o Many industries (e.g., finance, healthcare) have regulatory requirements that mandate continuous monitoring and reporting on model performance.
   - o Monitoring helps maintain compliance by producing logs and reports that detail model decisions, accuracy, and other relevant metrics.

6. **Error and Outlier Detection**:
   - o Unexpected inputs, or outliers, can lead models to produce incorrect predictions that might negatively impact business decisions.
   - o Monitoring for anomalies allows the model to either flag such cases for human review or trigger fallback mechanisms.

7. **Resource Management**:
   - o Monitoring also involves tracking resource usage, such as compute power, memory, and

storage, which is essential for optimizing costs and improving model efficiency.

o By analyzing resource metrics, organizations can refine their deployment strategies, scaling the model as needed and controlling costs.

How to Monitor Deployed Models

To achieve effective monitoring, organizations often implement specialized MLOps tools and frameworks. These tools track critical metrics and automate alerts when a model's performance or behavior deviates from expected norms. They may also facilitate:

- **Alerts and Notifications**: Automated alerts notify the team when key metrics (such as data drift, accuracy, latency) go out of acceptable bounds.
- **Retraining and Rollbacks**: Monitoring can trigger automated retraining workflows or roll back to a previous model version when performance declines significantly.
- **Dashboarding and Reporting**: Real-time dashboards provide clear visualizations of model metrics and historical trends, enabling teams to track changes over time.

Conclusion

Monitoring deployed ML models is essential for maintaining performance, fairness, and compliance over time. It empowers teams to proactively address issues, ensuring that the models continue to provide accurate and relevant predictions in a constantly changing environment. Effective monitoring safeguards the integrity and value of ML systems, enhancing both business outcomes and user trust.

Real-time Monitoring with Prometheus and Grafana

Real-time monitoring of machine learning models and associated systems is critical in MLOps. Prometheus and Grafana are two widely used open-source tools for implementing robust, real-time monitoring solutions. They provide detailed insights into model behavior, performance, and infrastructure, ensuring early detection of issues and continuous operation of deployed ML models.

Prometheus Overview

Prometheus is a time-series database and monitoring tool designed to collect, process, and store metric data from different services. It was developed by SoundCloud and is especially known for its efficient metric collection and alerting capabilities.

- **Metric Collection**: Prometheus uses a "pull" model to scrape metrics from target applications at set intervals. It collects data such as request rates, error rates, latency, and resource usage.
- **Multi-dimensional Data Model**: Prometheus stores metrics as time-series data with labels, allowing for powerful querying and filtering.
- **Alerting**: Prometheus can be configured with alerting rules based on specified thresholds or conditions. When an alert is triggered, it can notify team members via email, Slack, or other messaging platforms.
- **Data Retention**: Prometheus stores data locally and provides retention options, though it can be paired with remote storage solutions for extended retention.

Grafana Overview

Grafana is a visualization tool that integrates with Prometheus (and other data sources) to create interactive and informative dashboards.

- **Dashboards**: Grafana provides a user-friendly interface for visualizing data from Prometheus, allowing users to build custom dashboards for real-time monitoring.
- **Flexible Querying**: With its query editor, Grafana enables users to build complex queries, set filters, and analyze Prometheus data effectively.
- **Alerting Integration**: Grafana's built-in alerting allows alerts to be configured on visualized metrics, supplementing Prometheus's alert system.
- **Customizable Visuals**: It supports various visualizations such as line charts, heatmaps, and bar charts, which can be customized for model and infrastructure monitoring.

Setting Up Real-time Monitoring

1. Installing Prometheus and Grafana

- Both tools can be installed on-premises or deployed in cloud environments using Docker or Kubernetes.
- Set up Prometheus to scrape metrics from various endpoints, which could include your model server, APIs, or infrastructure.

2. Configuring Prometheus for Model Metrics

- Model metrics can be configured to include latency, accuracy, request rates, data drift indicators, and resource usage.
- Define custom metrics within your ML model service code, using Prometheus client libraries for Python, Java, or Go.

3. Creating Dashboards in Grafana

- Connect Grafana to Prometheus as a data source and design dashboards that visualize key model and infrastructure metrics.
- Create panels for metrics like request latency, error rates, model accuracy, memory usage, and data drift indicators to observe real-time model health.

4. Setting Up Alerts

- Alerts in Prometheus and Grafana can be configured to notify you of anomalies like sudden drops in accuracy, latency spikes, or increased resource consumption.
- Define alerting thresholds for each metric, and configure integrations to notify team members through various channels.

Example: Monitoring Model Inference Latency

1. **Instrument the Model Code**:

```
from prometheus_client import start_http_server, Summary

import time



# Create a metric to track latency

REQUEST_LATENCY = Summary('inference_latency_seconds', 'Time spent in model inference')



@REQUEST_LATENCY.time()

def predict():

    # Simulate model inference time

time.sleep(0.5)  # Replace with actual model inference code



if __name__ == '__main__':
```

```
start_http_server(8000)

while True:

predict()
```

2. **Query in Grafana**:
    1. Use Prometheus queries (e.g., rate(inference_latency_seconds[5m])) to analyze the metric data.
    2. Visualize the metrics with line charts to monitor latency over time.
3. **Configure Alerts**:
    1. Set up alerts in Prometheus, with conditions such as latency exceeding certain thresholds.
    2. Create Grafana alerts to trigger notifications when performance anomalies occur.

Conclusion

Real-time monitoring with Prometheus and Grafana enables proactive detection and mitigation of issues in deployed ML models, improving system reliability and model performance. Together, they form a powerful solution for monitoring, alerting, and visualizing the health and behavior of machine learning workflows.

Model Performance Metrics and Logging in MLOps

Monitoring and logging model performance metrics are essential parts of the machine learning lifecycle, particularly when deploying models to production. These practices help teams observe how well a model is performing, understand trends in accuracy, and detect anomalies. In MLOps, logging enables the collection of vital information for model improvement, debugging, and auditing, and can be configured to provide real-time insights into the behavior of the model in production.

Key Metrics for Model Performance

1. **Accuracy**: Proportion of correct predictions made by the model. This is commonly used in classification tasks.
2. **Precision**: The ratio of true positives to the sum of true positives and false positives. Precision is important in scenarios where false positives are costly.
3. **Recall**: The ratio of true positives to the sum of true positives and false negatives, often crucial for tasks where missing a positive instance is costly.
4. **F1 Score**: The harmonic mean of precision and recall, providing a balance between the two.
5. **ROC-AUC**: The area under the Receiver Operating Characteristic curve, often used to measure performance across all classification thresholds.
6. **Mean Absolute Error (MAE), Mean Squared Error (MSE)**: These are regression metrics for measuring error between predicted and actual values.
7. **Latency**: The time taken to generate a prediction, important for real-time systems.
8. **Throughput**: Number of predictions made per unit time, important for high-load environments.

Setting Up Metrics and Logging

1. Logging Framework Setup

Using Python's logging module, we can set up a centralized logging framework to capture metrics and other data points.

```
import logging
```

```
# Configure logging

logging.basicConfig(

    filename='model_performance.log',

    level=logging.INFO,
```

```
    format='%(asctime)s %(levelname)s %(message)s'
)

logger = logging.getLogger()
```

2. Implementing Model Performance Metrics Calculation

Below is an example of how to calculate performance metrics using scikit-learn in Python for a classification task.

```
from sklearn.metrics import accuracy_score,
precision_score, recall_score, f1_score, roc_auc_score

from sklearn.model_selection import train_test_split

from sklearn.ensemble import RandomForestClassifier

from sklearn.datasets import make_classification


# Generate sample data

X, y = make_classification(n_samples=1000,
n_features=20, random_state=42)

X_train, X_test, y_train, y_test = train_test_split(X, y,
test_size=0.2, random_state=42)


# Train a sample model

model = RandomForestClassifier()

model.fit(X_train, y_train)
```

```python
# Predictions

y_pred = model.predict(X_test)

y_proba = model.predict_proba(X_test)[:, 1]


# Calculating performance metrics

accuracy = accuracy_score(y_test, y_pred)

precision = precision_score(y_test, y_pred)

recall = recall_score(y_test, y_pred)

f1 = f1_score(y_test, y_pred)

roc_auc = roc_auc_score(y_test, y_proba)


# Log the performance metrics

logger.info(f"Accuracy: {accuracy}")

logger.info(f"Precision: {precision}")

logger.info(f"Recall: {recall}")

logger.info(f"F1 Score: {f1}")

logger.info(f"ROC AUC Score: {roc_auc}")
```

3. Adding Real-Time Logging for Model Inference

To monitor model performance in real-time, you can log metrics after each inference. Here's an example with inference latency logging:

```python
import time

import numpy as np


def predict(model, data):
start_time = time.time()

    predictions = model.predict(data)

    latency = time.time() - start_time

logger.info(f"Prediction latency: {latency} seconds")

    return predictions


# Example usage

sample_data = np.array([X_test[0]])  # Single data point

pred = predict(model, sample_data)
```

4. Real-Time Metric Collection with Prometheus (Optional)

For larger production systems, Prometheus can collect metrics at scale.

Install Prometheus Python client library:

```
pip install prometheus-client
```

Set up Prometheus metrics for latency:

```
from    prometheus_client    import    start_http_server,
Summary
```

```
# Define a metric for inference latency
```

```
LATENCY = Summary('inference_latency_seconds', 'Time spent
on inference')
```

```
@LATENCY.time()
```

```
def predict_with_latency(model, data):

    return model.predict(data)
```

```
# Start Prometheus server to expose metrics
```

```
start_http_server(8000)
```

```
# Make predictions and collect latency metrics
```

```
predictions = predict_with_latency(model, sample_data)
```

5. Structured Logging with JSON

For scalability, it's often useful to log data in a structured format like JSON, which can be parsed easily by log monitoring tools.

```
import json


def log_metrics(metrics):

    with open('model_metrics.json', 'a') as file:

json.dump(metrics, file)

file.write('\n')


# Sample metrics to log

metrics = {

    "accuracy": accuracy,

    "precision": precision,

    "recall": recall,

    "f1_score": f1,

    "roc_auc": roc_auc,

    "latency": latency

}

log_metrics(metrics)
```

Conclusion

Logging and tracking model performance metrics allow you to monitor a model's performance over time, identify potential issues, and ensure high-quality outputs in production. The example code demonstrates how to set up logging and real-time metric collection, providing a foundation for managing model performance in an MLOps pipeline.

Detecting Model Drift and Data Drift in MLOps

In production machine learning systems, model and data drift are significant issues that can degrade the performance of a model over time. Model drift occurs when the statistical properties of the target variable change, reducing the model's predictive accuracy. Data drift, on the other hand, happens when the input data distribution shifts, which can lead to a mismatch between training and production data. Detecting and addressing these drifts are key to maintaining model accuracy and reliability.

Types of Drift

1. **Model Drift**: Occurs when the relationship between input and output data shifts. This might happen if the target data changes or if new patterns emerge that were not in the training set.
2. **Data Drift**: Represents changes in the statistical properties of the input features. It includes:
   - **Covariate Drift**: Shift in the input feature distributions.
   - **Prior Probability Shift**: Change in the class distribution (common in classification tasks).
   - **Concept Drift**: Change in the relationship between input data and target variable.

Detecting Data Drift and Model Drift: Example with Python Code

Below is a step-by-step guide to implementing data drift and model drift detection.

1. Setting Up the Environment

Install required libraries:

pip install scikit-learn scipynumpy pandas

2. Generate a Simulated Dataset

To illustrate the concepts, we'll generate a synthetic dataset with initial data for model training and then simulate drift in the test data.

```
from sklearn.datasets import make_classification

from sklearn.model_selection import train_test_split

from sklearn.ensemble import RandomForestClassifier

import numpy as np

import pandas as pd



# Generate synthetic data

X, y = make_classification(n_samples=1000, n_features=20, random_state=42)

X_train, X_test, y_train, y_test = train_test_split(X, y, test_size=0.2, random_state=42)



# Train an initial model

model = RandomForestClassifier()

model.fit(X_train, y_train)
```

```
initial_preds = model.predict(X_test)
```

3. Data Drift Detection with Statistical Tests

The Kolmogorov-Smirnov (KS) test is a popular test for detecting changes in data distributions between training and production data.

```
from scipy.stats import ks_2samp
```

```
# Function to check data drift for each feature

def detect_data_drift(X_train, X_test, threshold=0.05):

drift_results = {}

    for col in range(X_train.shape[1]):

p_value = ks_2samp(X_train[:, col], X_test[:, col]).pvalue

drift_results[f'feature_{col}'] = p_value< threshold

    return drift_results
```

```
# Simulate drift by changing the distribution of some features in test data

X_test_drifted = X_test.copy()

X_test_drifted[:,    0]    +=    np.random.normal(0,    1,
X_test_drifted.shape[0])  # Add drift to feature 0
```

```
# Detect drift
```

```
data_drift_results = detect_data_drift(X_train, X_test_drifted)
```

```
print("Data Drift Results:", data_drift_results)
```

If the p-value is below the threshold (0.05), the feature is considered to have drifted.

4. Model Drift Detection with Concept Drift Monitoring

Concept drift can be monitored by checking the consistency in model predictions over time. Here, we use accuracy as a performance metric, but it could be any suitable metric for your model.

```
from sklearn.metrics import accuracy_score
```

```
# Measure initial model performance
```

```
initial_accuracy = accuracy_score(y_test, initial_preds)
```

```
# Simulate concept drift by changing the labels in the test set
```

```
y_test_drifted = y_test.copy()
```

```
flip_indices    =    np.random.choice(range(len(y_test_drifted)), size=50, replace=False)
```

```
y_test_drifted[flip_indices] = 1 - y_test_drifted[flip_indices]  # Flip some labels
```

```
# Evaluate the model on drifted data
```

```
drifted_preds = model.predict(X_test)
```

```
drifted_accuracy = accuracy_score(y_test_drifted, drifted_preds)


# Calculate accuracy drop to check for model drift

accuracy_drop = initial_accuracy - drifted_accuracy

print(f"Initial Accuracy: {initial_accuracy:.4f}, Drifted Accuracy: {drifted_accuracy:.4f}, Accuracy Drop: {accuracy_drop:.4f}")


if accuracy_drop> 0.05:  # Threshold for drift detection

print("Model drift detected")

else:

print("No significant model drift detected")
```

5. Automated Drift Monitoring and Alerts

In production, you would set up automated monitoring and alerting for drift detection. Tools like Grafana and Prometheus can be used to visualize and alert on changes in drift metrics.

Summary

Detecting data and model drift is essential for maintaining model performance. The code examples show how to detect data drift using statistical tests and model drift by monitoring performance metrics like accuracy.

Chapter-10 Model Retraining and Continuous Learning

When to Retrain Machine Learning Models

Retraining machine learning models is a crucial part of maintaining an effective ML system. As the data distribution changes over time, model accuracy and relevance can degrade, which can lead to poor performance and decision-making. Knowing when to retrain is essential to balance model accuracy and the computational costs of retraining.

Key Scenarios for Model Retraining

1. **Scheduled Retraining**: Retraining at regular intervals based on anticipated data changes.
2. **Performance Drop**: When the model's accuracy or other performance metrics fall below a certain threshold.
3. **Concept Drift and Data Drift**: Significant changes in the input data or relationships between inputs and outputs.

4. **New Data Availability**: Access to new or more comprehensive data can improve the model's generalization.
5. **Business Requirements**: Business changes, regulatory updates, or new customer requirements may necessitate updates in the model.

Code Example: Monitoring Model Performance to Trigger Retraining

Below is a sample implementation to detect when to retrain a model based on data drift and model performance metrics.

Setting Up the Environment

pip install scikit-learn numpy pandas

Step 1: Initial Model Training

We'll start by generating a dataset and training an initial model. This will be used as our baseline.

```
from sklearn.datasets import make_classification

from sklearn.model_selection import train_test_split

from sklearn.ensemble import RandomForestClassifier

from sklearn.metrics import accuracy_score


# Generate synthetic data

X, y = make_classification(n_samples=1000, n_features=20, random_state=42)

X_train, X_test, y_train, y_test = train_test_split(X, y, test_size=0.2, random_state=42)


# Initial model training
```

```
model = RandomForestClassifier()
model.fit(X_train, y_train)


# Evaluate initial model performance
initial_preds = model.predict(X_test)
initial_accuracy = accuracy_score(y_test, initial_preds)
print(f"Initial Model Accuracy: {initial_accuracy:.4f}")
```

Step 2: Setting up Drift Detection and Retraining Criteria

Define functions for data drift detection and model performance monitoring. Here, we use a Kolmogorov-Smirnov (KS) test to detect data drift and accuracy drop for performance monitoring.

```
from scipy.stats import ks_2samp
import numpy as np


# Function to check for data drift using KS test
def detect_data_drift(X_train, X_test, threshold=0.05):
drift_results = {}
   for col in range(X_train.shape[1]):
p_value = ks_2samp(X_train[:, col], X_test[:, col]).pvalue
drift_results[f'feature_{col}'] = p_value< threshold
   return drift_results


# Function to check model performance
def      should_retrain(initial_accuracy,      current_accuracy,
accuracy_drop_threshold=0.05):
```

accuracy_drop = initial_accuracy - current_accuracy

    return accuracy_drop>accuracy_drop_threshold

Step 3: Simulate Drift and Monitor Performance

To simulate real-world conditions, we create drifted data and check if retraining is required.

```
# Simulate drift in test data

X_test_drifted = X_test.copy()

X_test_drifted[:,    0]    +=    np.random.normal(0,    1,
X_test_drifted.shape[0])  # Add drift to feature 0


# Detect data drift

data_drift_results = detect_data_drift(X_train, X_test_drifted)

print("Data Drift Results:", data_drift_results)


# Evaluate model on drifted data

drifted_preds = model.predict(X_test_drifted)

drifted_accuracy = accuracy_score(y_test, drifted_preds)

print(f"Drifted Model Accuracy: {drifted_accuracy:.4f}")


# Check if retraining is needed based on accuracy drop

if should_retrain(initial_accuracy, drifted_accuracy):

print("Retraining Required: Significant accuracy drop detected.")

else:

print("No retraining required: Model accuracy is stable.")
```

Step 4: Automating Retraining

In a production setup, retraining would typically be automated within a pipeline using tools such as Kubeflow, Airflow, or MLflow. The following code represents a simplified approach to automated retraining:

```python
# Simplified retraining function

def retrain_model(X_train, y_train):

new_model = RandomForestClassifier()

new_model.fit(X_train, y_train)

print("Model retrained successfully.")

    return new_model


# Trigger retraining if required

if should_retrain(initial_accuracy, drifted_accuracy):

    model = retrain_model(X_train, y_train)

    # After retraining, re-evaluate the model to update the initial accuracy

initial_preds = model.predict(X_test_drifted)

initial_accuracy = accuracy_score(y_test, initial_preds)

print(f"New Model Accuracy after Retraining: {initial_accuracy:.4f}")

else:

print("Retraining was not triggered.")
```

Summary

This code demonstrates a basic workflow for monitoring and retraining machine learning models when performance drops or data drift is detected. By establishing thresholds for accuracy and monitoring data distribution, you can ensure models stay accurate and robust over time.

Automating Model Retraining Pipelines

Automating model retraining pipelines in MLOps involves setting up workflows that automatically detect conditions requiring retraining and then triggering the retraining process. This ensures models stay current without requiring manual intervention. We'll walk through creating an automated retraining pipeline using a simplified framework with Python and common tools for orchestration like Airflow.

Overview of Automated Retraining Pipeline

1. **Model Monitoring**: Track model performance and data drift in production.
2. **Data Versioning**: Track data changes to detect significant variations.
3. **Triggering Retraining**: Automatically trigger retraining when performance drops or data drift occurs.
4. **Model Training and Evaluation**: Retrain and evaluate the model on updated data.
5. **Deployment**: Replace the old model with the new one if it performs better.
6. **Continuous Integration with CI/CD**: Integrate with tools like Jenkins or GitLab for deployment.

Example Pipeline Implementation

Below is an example of automating a retraining pipeline. We'll use **Airflow** for orchestration and **MLflow** for model tracking.

Prerequisites

Install the necessary libraries:

pip install apache-airflow mlflow scikit-learn pandas

Step 1: Setting Up Airflow for Orchestration

Airflow helps to schedule and manage tasks in the retraining pipeline. Here's how to set up a simple DAG (Directed Acyclic Graph) that checks for drift, retrains the model if necessary, and updates the model registry.

Airflow DAG for Model Retraining (retraining_pipeline_dag.py):

```python
from airflow import DAG

from airflow.operators.python import PythonOperator

from datetime import datetime, timedelta

from mlflow.tracking import MlflowClient

import mlflow

from your_ml_module import check_data_drift, retrain_model, evaluate_model


# Define default arguments
default_args = {

    'owner': 'airflow',

    'retries': 1,

    'retry_delay': timedelta(minutes=5),

    'start_date': datetime(2023, 1, 1),

}


# Initialize Airflow DAG
```

```
dag = DAG(
   'model_retraining_pipeline',
default_args=default_args,
   description='Automated model retraining pipeline',
schedule_interval='@daily',  # Adjust as needed
)


# Define the task to check for data drift
def monitor_drift(**kwargs):
drift_detected = check_data_drift()
   return drift_detected


# Define the task to retrain the model
def retrain_and_log_model(**kwargs):
mlflow.start_run()
   model = retrain_model()
   accuracy = evaluate_model(model)
mlflow.log_metric("accuracy", accuracy)
mlflow.sklearn.log_model(model, "model")
mlflow.end_run()
   return accuracy


# Airflow tasks
drift_task = PythonOperator(
task_id='check_data_drift',
```

```
python_callable=monitor_drift,

provide_context=True,

dag=dag,

)


retrain_task = PythonOperator(

task_id='retrain_model',

python_callable=retrain_and_log_model,

provide_context=True,

dag=dag,

)


# Setting task dependencies

drift_task>>retrain_task
```

Step 2: Data Drift Detection

Data drift detection is essential to determine whether model retraining is necessary. You might use a statistical method (e.g., Kolmogorov-Smirnov test) to compare training and current data distributions. Here's an example function:

```
from scipy.stats import ks_2samp

import pandas as pd


def check_data_drift():

training_data = pd.read_csv('training_data.csv')

production_data = pd.read_csv('production_data.csv')
```

```
drift_detected = False

    for column in training_data.columns:

        stat,    p_value    =    ks_2samp(training_data[column],
production_data[column])

        if p_value< 0.05:  # Adjust threshold as needed

drift_detected = True

            break


    return drift_detected
```

Step 3: Model Retraining and Evaluation

Define functions to retrain and evaluate the model. Retraining could involve re-running the entire model training pipeline on the latest data.

```
from sklearn.ensemble import RandomForestClassifier

from sklearn.metrics import accuracy_score

import pandas as pd


# Retrain model with latest data

def retrain_model():

    data = pd.read_csv('updated_training_data.csv')

    X = data.drop('target', axis=1)

    y = data['target']


    model = RandomForestClassifier()
```

```
model.fit(X, y)
    return model


# Evaluate model
def evaluate_model(model):
test_data = pd.read_csv('test_data.csv')
X_test = test_data.drop('target', axis=1)
y_test = test_data['target']


    preds = model.predict(X_test)
    accuracy = accuracy_score(y_test, preds)
    return accuracy
```

Step 4: Register and Deploy Model

Using MLflow, you can register and manage model versions to handle production deployment seamlessly.

```
import mlflow
from mlflow.tracking import MlflowClient


def register_and_deploy_model(model, accuracy):
mlflow.log_metric("accuracy", accuracy)
model_uri = "runs:/"+mlflow.active_run().info.run_id+"/model"
    client = MlflowClient()


    # Register the model version
model_version = client.create_model_version(
```

```python
    name="RandomForestModel",

    source=model_uri,

run_id=mlflow.active_run().info.run_id

    )


    # Transition to production stage
client.transition_model_version_stage(

    name="RandomForestModel",

    version=model_version.version,

    stage="Production"

    )
```

Step 5: Complete Airflow DAG with Conditional Retraining

The final step is to include conditional checks in the Airflow pipeline to trigger retraining only when drift is detected.

```python
from airflow.operators.python import BranchPythonOperator


# Branch task to decide whether to retrain

def decide_to_retrain(**kwargs):

drift_detected                                    =
kwargs['ti'].xcom_pull(task_ids='check_data_drift')

    if drift_detected:

        return 'retrain_model'

    return 'no_op'


decide_task = BranchPythonOperator(
```

```
task_id='decide_to_retrain',

python_callable=decide_to_retrain,

provide_context=True,

dag=dag,

)


no_op_task = PythonOperator(

task_id='no_op',

python_callable=lambda: print("No retraining necessary."),

dag=dag,

)


# Update dependencies

drift_task>>decide_task

decide_task>> [retrain_task, no_op_task]
```

Summary

This automated retraining pipeline performs the following steps:

1. **Data Drift Detection**: Detects drift to decide whether retraining is necessary.
2. **Conditional Retraining**: Triggers retraining only when drift is detected.
3. **Logging and Model Versioning**: Tracks model performance and registers model versions using MLflow.
4. **Orchestration with Airflow**: Automates the retraining pipeline on a scheduled basis or upon specific conditions.

With this setup, your model retraining pipeline can run independently, ensuring your model remains accurate and reliable over time without manual intervention.

Feedback Loops and Continuous Improvement

Implementing feedback loops and continuous improvement is essential for maintaining the quality and relevance of machine learning models over time. This process involves collecting real-time feedback on the model's predictions, analyzing it, and using it to adjust the model, retrain it, or refine the data. Here's an in-depth guide on setting up a feedback loop and continuous improvement pipeline with code examples.

Steps in Feedback Loop and Continuous Improvement

1. **Collect Real-Time Feedback**: Capture feedback from model predictions in production.
2. **Analyze Feedback**: Use analytics to identify areas for improvement.
3. **Data Refinement**: Refine training data with feedback to improve data quality.
4. **Model Retraining**: Retrain the model on updated data.
5. **Deploy the Updated Model**: Continuously integrate and deploy improved models.

Example Workflow

We'll use Python and tools like **MLflow** for tracking, **Airflow** for orchestration, and **Flask** to simulate a feedback API. This setup will allow real-time feedback collection, analysis, and model improvement.

Step 1: Setting Up Real-Time Feedback Collection

Assume that we have a deployed model in production, and we want to collect feedback from users about the model's predictions.

Flask API for Feedback Collection

This API will capture user feedback on model predictions. Feedback data (e.g., prediction correctness) is stored in a database or file system for analysis.

```python
from flask import Flask, request, jsonify

import json


app = Flask(__name__)


@app.route('/predict', methods=['POST'])

def predict():

    data = request.get_json()

    # Mock prediction; replace with actual model inference

    prediction = "positive" if data['input'] > 0.5 else "negative"

    response = {"prediction": prediction}

    return jsonify(response)


@app.route('/feedback', methods=['POST'])

def feedback():

    data = request.get_json()

    with open('feedback_data.json', 'a') as f:
```

```
json.dump(data, f)

f.write("\n")

    return jsonify({"status": "Feedback recorded"})


if __name__ == '__main__':

app.run(port=5000)
```

- **Endpoint /predict**: Receives inputs, makes predictions, and returns results.
- **Endpoint /feedback**: Captures user feedback on the prediction. Here, feedback is stored in a file, but it could also be saved to a database.

Step 2: Analyzing Feedback

Analyze feedback periodically to identify model performance trends, data drift, or biases. This example uses a simple script to read the feedback file and generate insights.

```
import json

from collections import Counter


def analyze_feedback():

    with open('feedback_data.json', 'r') as f:

feedback_records = [json.loads(line) for line in f]


correct_predictions = [rec for rec in feedback_records if rec['feedback'] == 'correct']

incorrect_predictions = [rec for rec in feedback_records if rec['feedback'] == 'incorrect']
```

```
accuracy = len(correct_predictions) / len(feedback_records) *
100 if feedback_records else 0
```

```
print("Feedback Summary:")

print(f"Total records: {len(feedback_records)}")

print(f"Correct predictions: {len(correct_predictions)}")

print(f"Incorrect predictions: {len(incorrect_predictions)}")

print(f"Accuracy from feedback: {accuracy:.2f}%")
```

```
analyze_feedback()
```

Step 3: Data Refinement and Retraining Pipeline

Use feedback to refine data and create a retraining pipeline that leverages the improved data.

Feedback Data Processing

Here's an example script to process feedback data, filtering and preparing it for retraining. We can append this processed feedback to our training data.

```
import pandas as pd
```

```
def process_feedback_data():
    # Load feedback
feedback_df = pd.read_json('feedback_data.json', lines=True)
```

```
    # Select incorrect predictions for data refinement
incorrect_df = feedback_df[feedback_df['feedback'] == 'incorrect']
```

```
# Augment incorrect predictions into the training set

# Assumes feedback_df has columns 'input' and 'target'

incorrect_df['target'] = incorrect_df['input'].apply(lambda x: 1 if x >
0.5 else 0)

incorrect_df[['input',
'target']].to_csv('augmented_training_data.csv',          mode='a',
header=False)


process_feedback_data()
```

Step 4: Model Retraining

Retrain the model periodically on the augmented dataset, including new feedback data. Here's an example of retraining using **scikit-learn**.

```
from sklearn.ensemble import RandomForestClassifier

from sklearn.metrics import accuracy_score

import pandas as pd

import mlflow


def retrain_model():
    # Load augmented data
    data = pd.read_csv('augmented_training_data.csv')
    X = data['input'].values.reshape(-1, 1)
    y = data['target'].values


    # Retrain model
```

```python
    model = RandomForestClassifier()
model.fit(X, y)


    # Log model in MLflow
mlflow.start_run()
mlflow.sklearn.log_model(model, "model")
mlflow.end_run()


    return model


retrained_model = retrain_model()
```

Step 5: Continuous Integration and Deployment

Using **Airflow**, schedule the feedback analysis and retraining tasks. This ensures feedback data is processed, retrained, and deployed as part of a continuous workflow.

Airflow DAG for Feedback Loop

```python
from airflow import DAG
from airflow.operators.python import PythonOperator
from datetime import datetime, timedelta


default_args = {
    'owner': 'airflow',
    'start_date': datetime(2023, 1, 1),
    'retries': 1,
    'retry_delay': timedelta(minutes=5),
```

```
}

dag = DAG(
    'feedback_loop_pipeline',
default_args=default_args,
    description='Feedback loop and retraining pipeline',
schedule_interval='@daily',
)


feedback_analysis_task = PythonOperator(
task_id='analyze_feedback',
python_callable=analyze_feedback,
dag=dag,
)


data_refinement_task = PythonOperator(
task_id='process_feedback_data',
python_callable=process_feedback_data,
dag=dag,
)


retrain_model_task = PythonOperator(
task_id='retrain_model',
python_callable=retrain_model,
dag=dag,
```

)

Define the pipeline sequence

feedback_analysis_task>>data_refinement_task>>retrain_model_task

Summary

This pipeline demonstrates a complete feedback loop for continuous model improvement:

1. **Real-Time Feedback Collection**: Collect user feedback through a REST API.
2. **Feedback Analysis**: Periodically analyze feedback to gauge model performance.
3. **Data Refinement**: Use feedback to improve training data quality.
4. **Automated Retraining**: Periodically retrain the model on improved data.
5. **Continuous Deployment**: Automate deployment with tools like Airflow.

This approach ensures the model adapts to new data and user feedback, maintaining high performance and relevancy in production.

Handling Changes in Data Distribution

Handling changes in data distribution, or **data drift**, is critical in maintaining the performance of machine learning models over time. Data drift occurs when the statistical properties of input data change, leading to decreased model accuracy. Identifying, monitoring, and mitigating drift allows us to update or retrain models in response to evolving data.

This guide provides code and steps to detect, analyze, and handle changes in data distribution using tools like Python and scikit-learn.

Steps to Handle Data Drift

1. **Detecting Data Drift**: Identify when the distribution of new data differs from the training data.
2. **Analyzing Data Drift**: Quantify the drift and determine if retraining is required.
3. **Mitigating Data Drift**: Retrain the model or adjust its parameters.
4. **Monitoring Continuously**: Automate monitoring to detect drift in real-time.

Step 1: Detecting Data Drift

One common method for drift detection is the **Kolmogorov-Smirnov (KS) Test**, which compares the distributions of the training data and new data.

Example Code for Data Drift Detection

Let's start by defining a function to check for data drift using the KS test.

```
import pandas as pd

import numpy as np

from scipy.stats import ks_2samp


def detect_data_drift(train_data, new_data, threshold=0.05):

drift_detected = {}

    for column in train_data.columns:

        # Perform KS test on each feature
```

```
    stat,    p_value    =    ks_2samp(train_data[column],
new_data[column])
```

```
drift_detected[column] = p_value<threshold  # True if p-value is
below threshold
```

```
drifted_columns = [col for col, drift in drift_detected.items() if drift]
```

```
print(f"Drift detected in columns: {drifted_columns}")
```

```
    return drifted_columns
```

```
# Example usage
```

```
train_data = pd.DataFrame({'feature1': np.random.normal(0, 1,
1000), 'feature2': np.random.normal(0, 1, 1000)})
```

```
new_data = pd.DataFrame({'feature1': np.random.normal(0.5, 1,
1000), 'feature2': np.random.normal(0, 1, 1000)})
```

```
drifted_columns = detect_data_drift(train_data, new_data)
```

- **Output**: The function prints columns where data drift is detected, based on a significance threshold.

Step 2: Quantifying Data Drift

To understand the extent of data drift, we can use metrics like the **Jensen-Shannon (JS) Divergence** or **Population Stability Index (PSI)**. Here's an example with PSI.

Population Stability Index (PSI) Calculation

```
def calculate_psi(expected, actual, buckets=10):
```

```
    # Create bins and compute histograms
```

```
    breakpoints = np.linspace(0, 1, buckets + 1)
```

```python
expected_percents = np.histogram(expected, bins=breakpoints)[0] / len(expected)

actual_percents = np.histogram(actual, bins=breakpoints)[0] / len(actual)

# Calculate PSI

psi = np.sum((expected_percents - actual_percents) * np.log(expected_percents / actual_percents))

return psi


# Example usage

psi_feature1 = calculate_psi(train_data['feature1'], new_data['feature1'])

psi_feature2 = calculate_psi(train_data['feature2'], new_data['feature2'])


print(f"PSI for feature1: {psi_feature1}")

print(f"PSI for feature2: {psi_feature2}")
```

- **Interpretation**: A higher PSI value typically indicates a greater drift, with values above 0.2 often suggesting significant changes in data distribution.

Step 3: Mitigating Data Drift

If data drift is detected, we can mitigate it by retraining or fine-tuning the model using new data.

Example of Retraining a Model with Drifted Data

Here's how you can set up an automated retraining function if drift is detected.

```python
from sklearn.ensemble import RandomForestClassifier
```

```
from sklearn.model_selection import train_test_split
from sklearn.metrics import accuracy_score


# Example data
X = train_data[['feature1', 'feature2']]
y = np.random.choice([0, 1], size=1000)


new_X = new_data[['feature1', 'feature2']]
new_y = np.random.choice([0, 1], size=1000)


# Initial model training
X_train, X_val, y_train, y_val = train_test_split(X, y,
test_size=0.2)
model = RandomForestClassifier()
model.fit(X_train, y_train)


# Calculate baseline performance
initial_accuracy = accuracy_score(y_val, model.predict(X_val))
print(f"Initial Validation Accuracy: {initial_accuracy:.2f}")


# Retrain if drifted columns are detected
if drifted_columns:
model.fit(new_X, new_y)
new_accuracy = accuracy_score(y_val, model.predict(X_val))
```

```python
print(f"Updated    Validation    Accuracy    after    Retraining:
{new_accuracy:.2f}")
```

Step 4: Continuous Monitoring with Automated Alerts

For real-time monitoring, integrate the drift detection function into a **scheduled pipeline** using tools like **Airflow**. This pipeline can trigger alerts when drift is detected.

Airflow DAG for Continuous Drift Monitoring

```python
from airflow import DAG

from airflow.operators.python import PythonOperator

from datetime import datetime, timedelta


default_args = {
    'owner': 'airflow',
    'start_date': datetime(2023, 1, 1),
    'retries': 1,
    'retry_delay': timedelta(minutes=10),
}


dag = DAG(
    'data_drift_monitoring',
default_args=default_args,
    description='Monitoring data drift continuously',
schedule_interval=timedelta(hours=6),
)
```

```
detect_drift_task = PythonOperator(

task_id='detect_data_drift',

python_callable=detect_data_drift,

op_args=[train_data, new_data],

dag=dag,

)
```

This setup enables automated drift detection at regular intervals. When drift is detected, it could trigger retraining, model re-deployment, or alerts to a monitoring dashboard.

Summary

This workflow provides a robust method for handling changes in data distribution:

1. **Detection**: Identify significant shifts in feature distributions.
2. **Quantification**: Measure drift severity using metrics like PSI.
3. **Mitigation**: Retrain or adjust models as needed based on drift.
4. **Automation**: Implement continuous monitoring for proactive model management.

With these steps, you can ensure model performance remains stable even as input data evolves over time.

Chapter-11 Tools and Platforms for MLOps

Open Source MLOps Tools Overview

Open source tools have transformed MLOps, providing versatile, community-driven frameworks that help streamline and automate machine learning workflows. Let's break down the essential open-source MLOps tools: **MLflow**, **Kubeflow**, **TensorFlow Extended (TFX)**, and **Airflow**. Each has unique features suited for different stages of the machine learning lifecycle.

1. MLflow: Experiment Tracking and Model Management

MLflow is an open-source platform designed for managing the entire machine learning lifecycle, including experimentation, reproducibility, and deployment.

Key Components of MLflow:

- **MLflow Tracking**: Records and organizes experiment data (e.g., parameters, metrics, artifacts). This enables developers to track experiment details, making it easy to compare different model versions.

- **MLflow Projects**: Standardizes reproducibility through reusable, organized machine learning code. Projects are defined in MLproject files, which include environment specifications and run commands.
- **MLflow Models**: Offers a consistent model packaging format for deploying models across different frameworks (e.g., PyTorch, TensorFlow). It enables deploying models with tools like MLflow REST API, SageMaker, or Docker.
- **MLflow Model Registry**: Manages and organizes model versions. It includes model versioning, annotations, and lifecycle transitions, helping manage model deployments.

Example MLflow Workflow:

Here's how MLflow can be used for logging experiments.

```
import mlflow

import mlflow.sklearn

from sklearn.ensemble import RandomForestClassifier

from sklearn.datasets import load_iris

from sklearn.model_selection import train_test_split


# Load data

data = load_iris()

X_train, X_test, y_train, y_test = train_test_split(data.data, data.target, test_size=0.2, random_state=42)


# Experiment logging

with mlflow.start_run():

    model = RandomForestClassifier(n_estimators=50, random_state=42)
```

```
model.fit(X_train, y_train)
    accuracy = model.score(X_test, y_test)


    # Log metrics and parameters
mlflow.log_metric("accuracy", accuracy)
mlflow.log_param("n_estimators", 50)


    # Save model
mlflow.sklearn.log_model(model, "random_forest_model")
```

MLflow's flexibility with various ML frameworks, easy deployment integration, and tracking features make it highly valuable for experiment management.

2. Kubeflow: Orchestrating and Scaling ML Pipelines on Kubernetes

Kubeflow is a Kubernetes-based platform for deploying, managing, and scaling machine learning workflows.

Key Features of Kubeflow:

- **Pipeline Orchestration**: Kubeflow Pipelines allows the creation and execution of ML workflows using reusable components and supports tracking experiments and artifacts.
- **Scalability**: Built to leverage Kubernetes, Kubeflow supports distributed training and hyperparameter tuning across large clusters.
- **Jupyter Notebooks**: Provides integrated Jupyter notebooks, making data exploration and interactive development easy.
- **Model Serving**: Supports model deployment with KFServing, which enables easy API management for models in production.

Example Kubeflow Pipeline:

A simple Kubeflow pipeline is constructed by defining individual tasks (e.g., data preprocessing, training) as separate components.

```python
import kfp

from kfp import dsl


@dsl.pipeline(
    name='Simple ML Pipeline',
    description='A pipeline that demonstrates data preprocessing and model training'
)
def sample_pipeline():
    preprocess_op = dsl.ContainerOp(
        name='preprocess',
        image='your-preprocess-image',
        command=['python', 'preprocess.py']
    )
    train_op = dsl.ContainerOp(
        name='train',
        image='your-train-image',
        command=['python', 'train.py']
    ).after(preprocess_op)
```

Kubeflow excels at deploying production-level machine learning pipelines by offering an enterprise-scale solution for complex workflows.

3. TensorFlow Extended (TFX): End-to-End Pipeline for TensorFlow Models

TFX is an end-to-end platform tailored to deploying production-level TensorFlow pipelines, facilitating scalable, reliable machine learning deployments.

Key Components of TFX:

- **ExampleGen**: Ingests and splits data, an essential step for preparing data for machine learning workflows.
- **Transform**: Performs feature engineering, normalizing, and pre-processing data, allowing for reusable data transformations.
- **Trainer**: Configures and trains models using TensorFlow's robust deep learning capabilities.
- **Evaluator**: Measures model performance to validate accuracy and fairness before deployment.
- **Pusher**: Automatically deploys the model to a production environment if it meets performance criteria.

Example TFX Pipeline:

A TFX pipeline example where components work together to prepare, train, and deploy a model.

```
import tfx

from tfx.components import ExampleGen, Trainer, Evaluator, Pusher

from tfx.orchestration.experimental.interactive.interactive_context import InteractiveContext


# Initialize TFX context

context = InteractiveContext()
```

```
# Create TFX components

example_gen = ExampleGen(input=...)

trainer          =          Trainer(module_file='model_trainer.py',
examples=example_gen.outputs['examples'])

evaluator = Evaluator(examples=trainer.outputs['examples'])

pusher           =          Pusher(model=trainer.outputs['model'],
push_destination=...)


# Add components to pipeline

context.run(example_gen)

context.run(trainer)

context.run(evaluator)

context.run(pusher)
```

TFX's deep integration with TensorFlow is optimal for TensorFlow-focused projects that require detailed pipeline orchestration and production-ready data pipelines.

4. Airflow: Workflow Automation for Data and ML Pipelines

Apache Airflow is a platform for authoring, scheduling, and monitoring workflows. While not exclusively built for MLOps, it has become a popular choice for orchestrating ML pipelines.

Key Features of Airflow:

- **Task Orchestration**: Defines complex, directed acyclic graphs (DAGs) for data pipelines.
- **Flexible Scheduling**: Schedules tasks with a robust scheduling engine that supports complex dependencies.
- **Integrations**: Works well with other tools like MLflow, Kubernetes, and Spark, making it highly adaptable to various ML workflows.

- **Monitoring and Logging**: Provides extensive monitoring, logging, and alerting for all tasks in a pipeline.

Example Airflow DAG for ML Pipeline:

A sample DAG that preprocesses data, trains a model, and stores metrics.

```python
from airflow import DAG

from airflow.operators.python_operator import PythonOperator

from datetime import datetime


# Define your ML tasks
def data_preprocessing():
    # Data preprocessing logic
    pass


def model_training():
    # Model training logic
    pass


with DAG('ml_pipeline',
start_date=datetime(2023, 1, 1),
schedule_interval='@daily') as dag:


    preprocess_task = PythonOperator(
    task_id='data_preprocessing',
```

```
python_callable=data_preprocessing,

    )

train_task = PythonOperator(

task_id='model_training',

python_callable=model_training,

    )
```

```
preprocess_task>>train_task
```

Airflow's versatility and ease of integration make it ideal for automating various stages of ML and data workflows.

Summary

Each of these tools provides essential functionalities for managing ML operations:

- **MLflow** is excellent for experiment tracking and model management.
- **Kubeflow** leverages Kubernetes for scaling and orchestrating complex ML pipelines.
- **TFX** is perfect for end-to-end TensorFlow model deployment pipelines.
- **Airflow** offers flexible, robust workflow automation suited for diverse ML and data tasks.

Together, these tools form the backbone of a robust MLOps ecosystem, ensuring smooth, scalable, and automated machine learning operations from development through to production.

Cloud Platforms for MLOp

Cloud platforms provide robust, scalable environments for implementing MLOps (Machine Learning Operations) by offering services that cover the end-to-end machine learning lifecycle—from data preparation and training to deployment and monitoring. Three major cloud platforms—**AWS SageMaker**, **Google AI Platform**, and **Azure Machine Learning**—offer powerful solutions tailored for different stages of the MLOps workflow.

1. AWS SageMaker

AWS SageMaker is Amazon's fully managed service designed to facilitate the entire machine learning lifecycle, from building and training models to deploying them in production. SageMaker provides flexibility for beginners and experts alike and supports MLOps workflows by offering tools for data preparation, model training, tuning, and deployment.

Key Features of AWS SageMaker:

- **Data Preparation**: SageMaker Data Wrangler simplifies data preparation, supporting connections to various data sources (e.g., Amazon S3, RDS) and tools for data transformation and visualization.
- **Model Training and Tuning**: SageMaker offers managed Jupyter notebooks, which allow data scientists to experiment with models in an interactive environment. It also supports distributed training, and SageMaker Automatic Model Tuning helps optimize hyperparameters.
- **Model Deployment**: SageMaker makes deploying models in production easy with support for both real-time and batch inference. SageMaker Endpoints provide auto-scaling for production environments, and Amazon SageMaker Multi-Model Endpoints allow hosting multiple models under a single endpoint.
- **Monitoring and Debugging**: SageMaker Model Monitor detects and alerts on data drift and performance issues.

SageMaker Debugger helps identify bottlenecks and optimize model training.
- **Pipeline Automation**: AWS SageMaker Pipelines, a recent addition, is a workflow automation tool for orchestrating MLOps workflows. It provides pipeline templates and supports CI/CD for model development.

Example AWS SageMaker Workflow:

Here's an example SageMaker workflow for training and deploying a model.

```
import sagemaker

from sagemaker import get_execution_role

from sagemaker.sklearn import SKLearn


# Set up session and role

sagemaker_session = sagemaker.Session()

role = get_execution_role()


# Define estimator

sklearn_estimator = SKLearn(entry_point='train.py',

                role=role,

framework_version='0.23-1',

instance_count=1,

instance_type='ml.m5.large')
```

```
# Fit model

sklearn_estimator.fit({'train': 's3://mybucket/data/train.csv'})


# Deploy model to endpoint

predictor                                          =
sklearn_estimator.deploy(instance_type='ml.m5.large',
initial_instance_count=1)


# Make predictions

result = predictor.predict(data)

print(result)
```

AWS SageMaker excels in handling the full ML pipeline while integrating well with other AWS services, making it an ideal choice for organizations already using AWS.

2. Google AI Platform

Google AI Platform, part of Google Cloud, offers a suite of services for building, deploying, and managing machine learning models at scale. Known for its flexibility and ease of integration with popular open-source tools, it supports a wide array of ML frameworks (e.g., TensorFlow, PyTorch) and allows users to leverage Google's AI technology.

Key Features of Google AI Platform:

- **Data Preparation and Storage**: Google AI Platform connects easily with BigQuery, Google Cloud Storage, and Dataprep for handling data preprocessing, storage, and exploration tasks.

- **Model Training and Tuning**: Google AI Platform provides managed Jupyter notebooks, distributed training options, and integrated support for hyperparameter tuning. With Vertex AI, users can manage custom training jobs and auto-ML capabilities.
- **Model Deployment**: For deployment, AI Platform offers both online prediction (real-time) and batch prediction services. Vertex AI Endpoints simplify model versioning and scaling by managing different model versions for production.
- **Monitoring and Pipelines**: Google AI Platform Pipelines (Vertex AI Pipelines) use Kubernetes-based orchestration to build and deploy ML workflows. Vertex AI also provides automatic model monitoring, performance tracking, and alerts for data and concept drift.
- **AutoML**: Google's AutoML enables automatic training and tuning for users with less machine learning experience, delivering competitive models on custom datasets.

Example Google AI Platform Workflow:

Below is an example of training a model on Google AI Platform.

```
from google.cloud import aiplatform

from google.cloud.aiplatform import gapic as aiplatform_gapic


# Initialize AI Platform

aiplatform.init(project='my-project-id', location='us-central1')


# Define and train model
```

```
job = aiplatform.CustomTrainingJob(

display_name='my_training_job',

script_path='train.py',

container_uri='gcr.io/cloud-ml-algos/image',

model_serving_container_image_uri='gcr.io/cloud-ml-
algos/image'

)


model = job.run(

replica_count=1,

model_display_name='my_model',

args=['--data', 'gs://my-bucket/data']

)


# Deploy the model

endpoint = model.deploy(machine_type='n1-standard-4')
```

Google AI Platform is particularly suited for companies that want to leverage Google's advanced machine learning technology and integrate with Google Cloud's data tools.

3. Azure Machine Learning

Azure Machine Learning, Microsoft's fully managed service, helps organizations build, train, deploy, and manage machine learning models on Azure. The platform supports MLOps workflows with tools to automate and govern ML processes, from data processing to deployment.

Key Features of Azure Machine Learning:

- **Data Storage and Processing**: Azure ML integrates with Azure Data Lake, Blob Storage, and SQL Database, providing a centralized location for all data storage and preparation needs. Azure Data Prep helps with data wrangling and transformation.
- **Model Training and Tuning**: With Azure ML, users can conduct distributed training and hyperparameter tuning using managed or custom compute clusters. It also includes an integrated Jupyter notebook experience.
- **Model Deployment**: Azure ML allows model deployment to Azure Kubernetes Service (AKS), virtual machines, and Azure Functions for both real-time and batch inference. Azure also provides robust deployment monitoring capabilities.
- **Pipelines and CI/CD**: Azure ML Pipelines orchestrate end-to-end workflows with a modular approach that enables CI/CD integration. Azure DevOps supports creating repeatable workflows, and Azure ML allows for automated retraining and re-deployment based on new data or model performance changes.
- **Monitoring and Governance**: Azure ML's Model Monitor tracks data and concept drift. Azure also includes compliance and governance features, making it easier to meet industry standards and track model lineage.

Example Azure Machine Learning Workflow:

Here's an example of setting up a pipeline in Azure Machine Learning.

```
from azureml.core import Workspace, Experiment, ScriptRunConfig

from azureml.pipeline.core import Pipeline, PipelineData
```

```python
from azureml.pipeline.steps import PythonScriptStep


# Initialize Workspace

ws = Workspace.from_config()

experiment    =    Experiment(workspace=ws,    name='my-experiment')


# Define pipeline data

pipeline_data                =                PipelineData("output",
datastore=ws.get_default_datastore())


# Define steps

step1 = PythonScriptStep(

    name="data_processing",

script_name="data_processing.py",

    outputs=[pipeline_data],

compute_target="cpu-cluster",

source_directory="./scripts"

)

step2 = PythonScriptStep(

    name="model_training",
```

```
script_name="train.py",

  inputs=[pipeline_data],

compute_target="cpu-cluster",

source_directory="./scripts"

)



# Create and run pipeline

pipeline = Pipeline(workspace=ws, steps=[step1, step2])

pipeline_run = experiment.submit(pipeline)

pipeline_run.wait_for_completion()
```

Azure Machine Learning's strong integration with Azure DevOps and its compliance features make it a preferred choice for organizations with regulatory requirements or a need for structured workflow automation.

Summary

Each cloud platform has its strengths:

- **AWS SageMaker** offers an end-to-end MLOps solution with extensive integration across AWS services, making it a suitable option for large-scale workflows and extensive monitoring.
- **Google AI Platform** is highly flexible and integrates well with Google's data and AI technologies, making it ideal for projects that require advanced AutoML capabilities and Kubernetes support.
- **Azure Machine Learning** is excellent for organizations that need governance and compliance features and is

deeply integrated with Microsoft's broader suite, supporting enterprise-grade solutions.

Together, these platforms provide extensive MLOps functionality to streamline machine learning lifecycles, each tailored to meet the unique needs of enterprises across industries.

Chapter-12 MLOps Best Practices

Setting Up Reproducible ML Pipelines

Setting up reproducible ML pipelines is crucial in MLOps to ensure that machine learning experiments are consistent, traceable, and can be reliably rerun across different environments and over time. A reproducible pipeline captures the full lifecycle of a machine learning model, from data collection and preprocessing to model training, evaluation, and deployment. Here's a detailed breakdown of the steps involved in creating reproducible ML pipelines:

1. Define the ML Pipeline Stages

A reproducible ML pipeline should have clearly defined stages, which may include:

- **Data Collection and Ingestion**: Load and preprocess data from consistent sources.
- **Data Preprocessing**: Clean, transform, and prepare data, including handling missing values, normalizing, or scaling features.

- **Feature Engineering**: Generate or select features that improve model accuracy.
- **Model Training and Validation**: Train models with fixed configurations and track training metrics.
- **Model Evaluation**: Measure model performance using consistent metrics.
- **Model Deployment**: Push the model to production environments.
- **Monitoring**: Continuously track model performance to detect drift or degradation.

Each stage should be modular and self-contained, allowing individual stages to be run independently or collectively as part of a broader pipeline.

2. Environment Setup and Dependency Management

To achieve reproducibility, set up and maintain a consistent environment across different machines or cloud instances:

- **Use Virtual Environments**: Tools like virtualenv or conda allow you to manage dependencies within isolated environments.
- **Containerization**: Docker provides an effective way to package the pipeline code, dependencies, and environment settings into a consistent container image. This ensures that any machine with Docker installed can run the pipeline without version conflicts.
- **Package Management**: Define dependencies in requirements.txt for Python or use environment.yml for conda. Pin versions of libraries to prevent unexpected changes due to library updates.

Example requirements.txt:

scikit-learn==0.24.2

pandas==1.3.3

numpy==1.21.2

3. Data Versioning

Data versioning helps track changes to the datasets, ensuring that the same dataset version can be retrieved and used in future runs:

- **Version Control Systems**: Tools like DVC (Data Version Control) and Pachyderm manage data versions, allowing you to track changes to datasets.
- **Data Storage**: Use storage solutions like S3, Google Cloud Storage, or Azure Blob Storage that can be integrated with DVC, enabling you to store data versions and retrieve them as needed.

DVC Example:

```
# Initialize DVC in the project

dvcinit
```

```
# Track a dataset with DVC

dvc add data/raw_data.csv
```

```
# Commit the changes and push to remote storage

git add data/raw_data.csv.dvc

git commit -m "Track raw data with DVC"

dvc push
```

4. Code Versioning

Using version control for code ensures that every change is recorded, making it easier to reproduce or revert to previous versions of the pipeline:

- **Git**: Git is the most popular tool for versioning ML code. It allows you to create branches for experiments and track modifications with detailed commit histories.
- **Branching Strategy**: Adopt a branching strategy like Gitflow, where the main branch holds stable code, and branches are used for experimentation.

5. Experiment Tracking

Experiment tracking ensures that every experiment's parameters, metrics, and outputs are recorded for future reference and comparison:

- **MLflow, Weights & Biases, or TensorBoard**: These tools help track hyperparameters, metrics, and artifacts. Each experiment run is logged with unique identifiers, making it easy to compare model versions.
- **Logging Parameters and Metrics**: When training models, log all hyperparameters, metrics, and evaluation results to allow detailed comparison across experiments.

Example using MLflow:

```
import mlflow

import mlflow.sklearn



with mlflow.start_run():

    model = train_model()

    accuracy = evaluate_model(model)
```

\# Log metrics and parameters

mlflow.log_param("max_depth", 10)

mlflow.log_metric("accuracy", accuracy)

\# Save the model artifact

mlflow.sklearn.log_model(model, "model")

6. Pipeline Orchestration

Pipeline orchestration frameworks like **Apache Airflow**, **Kubeflow Pipelines**, and **Prefect** allow the management of complex ML workflows by enabling step dependencies, scheduling, and automatic retries for reproducibility.

- **Define Tasks and Dependencies**: Break down the pipeline into tasks, such as data ingestion, training, and deployment, with clear dependencies.
- **Scheduling and Automation**: Schedule pipelines to run at specified intervals, ensuring models are retrained or updated based on new data.

Example of an Airflow pipeline:

from airflow import DAG

from airflow.operators.python_operator import PythonOperator

from datetime import datetime

def preprocess_data():

```python
pass  # Data preprocessing logic


def train_model():

pass  # Model training logic


# Define DAG

with    DAG('ml_pipeline',    start_date=datetime(2023,    1,    1),
schedule_interval='@daily') as dag:

preprocess    =    PythonOperator(task_id='preprocess_data',
python_callable=preprocess_data)

    train    =    PythonOperator(task_id='train_model',
python_callable=train_model)


preprocess>>train  # Define task dependencies
```

7. Model Packaging and Deployment

Packaging the trained model ensures that it can be easily moved from the training environment to production:

- **Docker**: Package the trained model and its environment in a Docker container, which can then be deployed across different environments.
- **Model Serving Tools**: Use tools like Flask, FastAPI, or TensorFlow Serving to create REST APIs for serving models in production.

Example of packaging a model with Docker:

1. Create a Dockerfile:

```
FROM python:3.8-slim

# Copy files

COPY . /app

WORKDIR /app

# Install dependencies

RUN pip install -r requirements.txt

# Expose port

EXPOSE 5000

# Run the application

CMD ["python", "app.py"]
```

  2.   Build and run the Docker container:

```
docker build -t ml_model .

docker run -p 5000:5000 ml_model
```

8. Model and Data Monitoring

Monitoring deployed models ensures they continue to perform as expected, even as data distributions shift over time:

- **Model Performance Monitoring**: Use tools like Prometheus and Grafana to set up dashboards and alerts for tracking model performance metrics in production.
- **Data Drift Detection**: Implement mechanisms to detect drift by comparing incoming data distributions with training data distributions. Tools like Evidently AI can help in monitoring data drift.

Example using Prometheus and Grafana for monitoring:

- **Prometheus** collects model metrics (e.g., accuracy, latency) and stores them for analysis.
- **Grafana** visualizes these metrics with custom dashboards.

9. Documentation and Versioning for Reproducibility

Maintain detailed documentation and versioning for:

- **Pipeline Configurations**: Document configuration files with experiment parameters, pipeline settings, and deployment details.
- **Data Schemas**: Maintain schema versions to ensure that the pipeline handles changes in data structure over time.
- **Code Changes**: Keep detailed commit messages and tag production releases, making it easier to trace changes over time.

Summary

Creating reproducible ML pipelines requires careful management of the environment, data, code, and model versions. By implementing structured environments, data versioning, code tracking, experiment logging, and robust orchestration, you can ensure that machine learning experiments are fully reproducible and reliable across different scenarios.

Ensuring Scalability in MLOps

To ensure scalability in MLOps, the architecture and workflow need to be designed to handle increasing loads, model complexity, and growing datasets efficiently. Here are some strategies and practices for achieving scalability in MLOps:

1. Containerization and Microservices

- **Containerization**: Using Docker or other container technologies to package models and dependencies ensures consistency and allows models to be scaled and deployed across multiple environments.
- **Microservices**: Decompose monolithic applications into smaller, manageable services. Each service can be scaled independently, allowing for better load distribution and modularity.

2. Orchestrating Pipelines with Tools like Kubernetes and Kubeflow

- **Kubernetes**: Enables orchestration and scaling of containers across a cluster. It allows for dynamic scaling of resources based on demand, providing a foundation for handling fluctuating workloads.
- **Kubeflow**: Built on top of Kubernetes, Kubeflow allows for managing machine learning workflows. It provides an efficient way to deploy and scale models, train them on distributed systems, and automate the retraining and serving processes.

3. Automated Model Retraining and Continuous Integration/Continuous Deployment (CI/CD)

- **Automated Retraining**: Set up workflows to retrain models periodically or when data drift is detected. This ensures the model remains up-to-date with minimal manual intervention.

- **CI/CD**: Use CI/CD pipelines to automate testing, validation, and deployment of models. GitHub Actions, Jenkins, and GitLab CI/CD can automate testing and deployment, making scaling and version control more manageable.

4. Data Pipeline Scaling with Distributed Data Processing Frameworks

- **Apache Spark, Kafka, or Beam**: For large-scale data processing, use distributed data frameworks like Spark and Beam. They handle big data volumes and can process data in real-time or batch modes, making it easier to feed models at scale.
- **Data Lakes and Warehouses**: Set up a data lake (e.g., AWS S3, Azure Data Lake) or data warehouse (e.g., BigQuery, Snowflake) to store large datasets. This ensures seamless access to historical data, facilitating model retraining at scale.

5. Model Deployment Strategies

- **Model Serving**: Use dedicated model-serving frameworks like TensorFlow Serving, TorchServe, or FastAPI, optimized to handle high-throughput inference requests.
- **Load Balancing and A/B Testing**: Use load balancers to distribute incoming requests across multiple model instances. Implement A/B testing and canary deployments to evaluate models' performance and gradually scale the best-performing version.

6. Scalable Monitoring and Logging Solutions

- **Monitoring Tools**: Set up monitoring using Prometheus, Grafana, or ELK Stack to keep track of model performance, response time, and resource usage in real-time. Automated alerts help detect issues early.

- **Data and Model Drift Detection**: Use drift detection techniques (e.g., statistical tests, distribution monitoring) to catch changes in input data or model performance. Scalable monitoring allows for frequent checks without resource overuse.

7. Resource Scaling and Cost Optimization

- **Auto-scaling**: Cloud platforms (AWS, Azure, GCP) provide auto-scaling features to dynamically allocate resources based on demand. This helps in handling load spikes and optimizing cost.
- **Batch vs. Real-time Processing**: Prioritize real-time inference only when needed, and use batch processing for non-urgent tasks to optimize resource usage.

8. Using Feature Stores for Scalable Feature Management

- **Feature Stores**: Feature stores like Feast manage feature data across multiple models and datasets, ensuring consistency and versioning. They help in precomputing features for reuse, reducing redundancy, and accelerating model training and inference.

9. Versioning and Metadata Management with Model Registries

- **Model Registry**: Use a model registry (like MLflow, TFX) to track model versions, their metadata, and deployment history. This aids in scalability by making it easy to switch or update models across environments without major disruptions.

Implementing these practices ensures that your MLOps pipelines can handle increased loads and complexities while maintaining high availability and performance.

Managing Security and Compliance in ML Projects

Security and compliance in ML projects are essential to safeguard data, protect models from adversarial attacks, and ensure adherence to regulatory standards. Here are some best practices to manage these aspects effectively:

1. Data Security and Privacy

- **Data Encryption**: Encrypt data at rest and in transit. Use encryption standards such as AES-256 for storage and TLS for data transfers.
- **Anonymization and Pseudonymization**: Mask personally identifiable information (PII) using techniques like pseudonymization or k-anonymity. This minimizes risk exposure, especially in regulated industries.
- **Access Control**: Implement role-based access control (RBAC) and principle of least privilege (PoLP) to restrict data access only to authorized personnel. Use Multi-Factor Authentication (MFA) for additional security.

2. Model Security

- **Adversarial Attack Mitigation**: Defend against adversarial attacks (e.g., FGSM, PGD) by using techniques like adversarial training or gradient masking. Implement input sanitization to identify suspicious data inputs.
- **Model Encryption and Access Control**: Encrypt models and limit access to model artifacts. Only authorized users should have permissions to load, modify, or deploy models.
- **Watermarking**: Embed watermarks or unique signatures within models to identify ownership, which can deter model theft and help track unauthorized use.

3. Compliance with Data Regulations

- **GDPR and CCPA Compliance**: Ensure data processing practices comply with GDPR, CCPA, or other relevant regulations. This involves giving users control over their data, data deletion upon request, and transparency about data use.
- **Data Residency Requirements**: Some regulations mandate that data remains within specific geographic boundaries. Use cloud providers that support data residency controls to meet these requirements.

4. Secure Model Deployment

- **API Security**: Secure endpoints using API gateways and apply rate limiting to prevent abuse. Authentication tokens (e.g., OAuth) and request signatures (HMAC) help secure communication with models.
- **Network Security**: Use Virtual Private Networks (VPNs), Virtual Private Clouds (VPCs), and firewalls to restrict external access to model servers.
- **Runtime Monitoring**: Implement runtime monitoring to detect and respond to anomalous patterns in model requests or usage that might indicate security incidents.

5. Model Explainability and Interpretability for Compliance

- **Explainability Tools**: Use explainability frameworks (e.g., SHAP, LIME) to provide transparency in model decisions. This is crucial for compliance in industries where automated decision-making is regulated.
- **Model Audits**: Regularly audit models for fairness, transparency, and bias. Document how models make decisions and ensure stakeholders understand the decision-making process.

6. Data and Model Governance

- **Data Lineage**: Track and document data lineage to understand where data originates, how it's processed, and where it's used. This helps with traceability and compliance in case of audits.

- **Model Versioning and Audits**: Maintain a version history of models, including metadata on training data, hyperparameters, and evaluation metrics. This aids in tracing model versions and reproducing past results for audits.

7. Bias and Fairness Mitigation

- **Bias Testing**: Use fairness assessment tools (e.g., Fairness Indicators) to evaluate models for potential bias in predictions. Address biases related to sensitive attributes like age, gender, or race.
- **Fairness Constraints**: Implement constraints or re-sampling techniques during training to reduce bias. This can be especially relevant for models in finance, healthcare, and legal domains.

8. Logging and Monitoring for Security

- **Audit Logs**: Keep detailed logs of data access, model access, and API usage to trace back unauthorized actions or breaches.
- **Model Performance and Drift Monitoring**: Monitor for data drift and concept drift, which could indicate potential adversarial manipulation. Trigger alerts if drift or unexpected performance drops are detected.

9. Regular Penetration Testing and Vulnerability Assessments

- **Penetration Testing**: Conduct regular penetration testing to identify security loopholes in ML systems. Engage third-party security firms if needed to audit ML pipelines and detect vulnerabilities.
- **Dependency Management**: Regularly update and audit third-party libraries and frameworks to patch vulnerabilities. Automated dependency scanning tools can help identify outdated or vulnerable packages.

272

10. Incident Response and Recovery

- **Incident Response Plan**: Develop and rehearse an incident response plan specifically tailored to ML systems. This includes steps to handle model degradation, data breaches, or adversarial attacks.
- **Backup and Disaster Recovery**: Regularly back up models, data, and configuration settings. In the event of a security incident, a robust recovery strategy minimizes downtime and ensures continuity.

These strategies create a secure and compliant foundation for managing ML projects, from data ingestion and model training to deployment and monitoring.

Monitoring and Managing Model Lifecycle

Monitoring and managing the model lifecycle is essential to ensure that machine learning models remain accurate, reliable, and relevant over time. This lifecycle includes tracking model performance, detecting drift, managing versioning, and handling retraining needs. Here's a structured approach to managing the model lifecycle:

1. Model Development and Experiment Tracking

- **Experiment Tracking**: Track experiments, hyperparameters, model architectures, and results using tools like MLflow, Weights & Biases, or TensorBoard. This helps in comparing versions, tracking improvements, and selecting the best model for deployment.
- **Documentation**: Document model objectives, assumptions, and limitations. This is essential for future auditing and debugging.

2. Version Control

- **Data and Model Versioning**: Use tools like DVC (Data Version Control) and Git to version datasets, feature sets, and model artifacts. This enables reproducibility and allows you to roll back to previous versions when necessary.
- **Model Registry**: Maintain a model registry (e.g., MLflow, TFX Model Registry) to store different model versions, along with metadata such as training data, evaluation metrics, and deployment status.

3. Performance Monitoring in Production

- **Performance Metrics**: Continuously track model performance using metrics like accuracy, precision, recall, F1-score, and AUC-ROC. For regression models, track RMSE, MAE, and R-squared.
- **Real-time vs. Batch Monitoring**: Use real-time monitoring for critical metrics that could impact user experience (e.g., recommendation relevance) and batch monitoring for periodic evaluation of metrics that don't require instant action.

4. Data and Model Drift Detection

- **Data Drift**: Detect changes in the distribution of input data over time using statistical tests (e.g., Kolmogorov-Smirnov test, Chi-square test). Data drift often requires model retraining to maintain performance.
- **Concept Drift**: Monitor for concept drift, where the relationship between input features and the target variable changes. This can be detected by observing performance drops or using drift detection frameworks like Alibi Detect or River.

5. Model Retraining and Continuous Learning

- **Scheduled Retraining**: Set up automated retraining pipelines based on a predefined schedule (e.g., weekly, monthly) or when a certain performance threshold is breached.

- **Trigger-based Retraining**: Implement retraining triggers based on performance metrics, data drift, or concept drift. This approach enables models to adapt to changes without unnecessary retraining.
- **Continuous Learning Pipelines**: For high-velocity data (e.g., streaming data), design a continuous learning pipeline where the model is incrementally updated in response to new data.

6. Model Explainability and Interpretability

- **Interpretability Tools**: Use interpretability tools like SHAP, LIME, or Integrated Gradients to understand model predictions, especially when performance degrades. Interpretability helps identify possible issues related to feature importance or model bias.
- **Explainability in Monitoring**: Integrate explainability metrics into the monitoring process, ensuring stakeholders have insight into model decisions and changes over time.

7. Monitoring Infrastructure

- **Monitoring Tools**: Use monitoring tools like Prometheus, Grafana, or ELK Stack to set up real-time dashboards for model performance, latency, and system metrics.
- **Custom Alerts**: Configure custom alerts for threshold breaches (e.g., sudden accuracy drop, increased inference latency) to detect issues early. Alerts should be actionable and direct stakeholders to specific metrics that need attention.

8. Feedback Loop and Human-in-the-Loop (HITL) Systems

- **Feedback Collection**: Collect user feedback on model predictions to enhance model performance and identify errors. Customer feedback can provide insights into model weaknesses and areas for improvement.

- **Human-in-the-Loop**: For models requiring high accuracy, integrate HITL systems for reviewing model predictions, especially in areas like healthcare or finance, where prediction errors are costly.

9. Model Degradation Analysis and Retirement

- **Degradation Analysis**: Regularly analyze model degradation by comparing current performance metrics with initial benchmarks. Document reasons for degradation to inform future model updates.
- **Model Retirement**: Establish criteria for deprecating and retiring models that no longer meet performance standards or are obsolete due to new data patterns. Archive old models with their metadata for future reference.

10. Cost and Resource Optimization

- **Resource Usage Tracking**: Monitor resource usage (e.g., CPU, GPU, memory) to optimize cost, especially in cloud environments. Resource management tools can help in scaling up or down based on demand.
- **Cost-Effective Retraining**: Identify cost-effective retraining cycles based on data and concept drift rather than frequent retraining, which can consume excessive resources.

11. Auditability and Governance

- **Audit Logs**: Maintain logs of data usage, model training, and inference requests to support model traceability. This is critical for compliance and audits.
- **Governance Policies**: Develop policies that define roles, responsibilities, and workflows in model development, deployment, and monitoring. This ensures accountability and compliance across the ML lifecycle.

12. Testing and Validation in Production

- **Shadow Testing**: Before fully deploying a new model, conduct shadow testing by running it alongside the current model to compare predictions. This helps in detecting issues without affecting end-users.
- **A/B Testing and Canary Deployment**: Use A/B testing or canary deployment to gradually roll out new models and compare their performance with previous versions. This minimizes the impact of potential issues with the new model.

These practices help maintain model accuracy, reduce risk, and provide visibility into how models perform across their lifecycle. Effective lifecycle management ensures that ML models continue to provide value and reliability over time.

Chapter-13 Advanced MLOps Techniques

Automated Machine Learning (AutoML) Integration

Automated Machine Learning (AutoML) automates the process of model selection, hyperparameter tuning, and model evaluation, helping practitioners and businesses create optimized models quickly. AutoML can be integrated into the machine learning pipeline to streamline model building and enable non-experts to produce high-quality models. Here, we'll discuss various approaches to integrating AutoML with sample code using popular AutoML frameworks such as **Auto-sklearn**, **TPOT**, and **H2O.ai**.

1. AutoML Overview and Integration Steps

- **Data Preprocessing**: Ensure data is clean, balanced, and has no missing values.
- **Feature Engineering**: AutoML can often handle feature engineering, but domain-specific feature creation can enhance performance.

- **Model Selection**: AutoML automates model selection by testing multiple algorithms and picking the best-performing one.
- **Hyperparameter Tuning**: AutoML performs hyperparameter optimization to find the best parameters for the chosen models.
- **Model Evaluation and Deployment**: Once the best model is found, it can be evaluated on test data and deployed.

2. AutoML with Auto-sklearn

Auto-sklearn is a Python package built on scikit-learn and automates model selection, training, and hyperparameter tuning.

Installation on Bash

pip install auto-sklearn

Code Example python

```
import autosklearn.classification

from sklearn.model_selection import train_test_split

from sklearn.datasets import load_iris

from sklearn.metrics import accuracy_score


# Load and split the dataset

data = load_iris()

X_train, X_test, y_train, y_test = train_test_split(data.data, data.target, test_size=0.2, random_state=42)
```

```python
# Initialize AutoML classifier with time and ensemble size constraints

automl = autosklearn.classification.AutoSklearnClassifier(

    time_left_for_this_task=600,    # Total time in seconds for AutoML process

    per_run_time_limit=60,          # Time limit for each model training

    ensemble_size=50                # Number of models in the final ensemble

)


# Fit the model

automl.fit(X_train, y_train)


# Evaluate on test data

y_pred = automl.predict(X_test)

accuracy = accuracy_score(y_test, y_pred)

print(f"AutoML Model Accuracy: {accuracy * 100:.2f}%")


# Display the models used in the final ensemble

print(automl.show_models())
```

3. AutoML with TPOT

TPOT (Tree-based Pipeline Optimization Tool) uses genetic programming to find optimal ML pipelines.

Installation on Bash

pip install tpot

Code Example python

```python
from tpot import TPOTClassifier
from sklearn.model_selection import train_test_split
from sklearn.datasets import load_digits
from sklearn.metrics import accuracy_score


# Load and split the dataset
data = load_digits()
X_train, X_test, y_train, y_test = train_test_split(data.data,
data.target, test_size=0.2, random_state=42)


# Initialize TPOT classifier
tpot = TPOTClassifier(
    generations=5,          # Number of iterations to optimize the
pipeline
    population_size=20,     # Number of pipelines in each
generation
    verbosity=2,       # Level of verbosity for tracking progress
    random_state=42
)
```

```python
# Fit the model
tpot.fit(X_train, y_train)
```

```python
# Evaluate on test data
y_pred = tpot.predict(X_test)
accuracy = accuracy_score(y_test, y_pred)
print(f"TPOT Model Accuracy: {accuracy * 100:.2f}%")
```

```python
# Export the best model pipeline
tpot.export('best_tpot_pipeline.py')
```

The generated Python file (best_tpot_pipeline.py) contains the final, optimized model pipeline, which can be loaded and used independently.

4. AutoML with H2O.ai

H2O.ai provides a robust AutoML framework that supports both classification and regression, including automatic feature engineering, model ensembling, and hyperparameter tuning.

Installation on Bash

```bash
pip install h2o
```

Code Example python

```python
import h2o
from h2o.automl import H2OAutoML
from sklearn.datasets import load_wine
from sklearn.model_selection import train_test_split
```

```python
import pandas as pd

# Initialize H2O and load the dataset
h2o.init()
data = load_wine()
X_train, X_test, y_train, y_test = train_test_split(data.data,
data.target, test_size=0.2, random_state=42)


# Convert data to H2OFrame format
train_df         =          h2o.H2OFrame(pd.DataFrame(X_train,
columns=data.feature_names).assign(target=y_train))

test_df         =          h2o.H2OFrame(pd.DataFrame(X_test,
columns=data.feature_names).assign(target=y_test))


# Define feature names and target column
x = data.feature_names
y = 'target'


# Initialize and train AutoML
aml = H2OAutoML(max_runtime_secs=600, seed=42)   # Limit
the AutoML process to 10 minutes
aml.train(x=x, y=y, training_frame=train_df)


# Get the best model and performance
leader_model = aml.leader
perf = leader_model.model_performance(test_df)
```

```
print(perf)
```

```
# Predict on new data

predictions = leader_model.predict(test_df)

print(predictions.head())
```

5. AutoML with Google Cloud AutoML

Google Cloud AutoML provides AutoML capabilities for cloud environments, especially for large-scale applications.

Code Example (requires Google Cloud account setup)

```
from google.cloud import automl_v1beta1 as automl


# Initialize AutoML client and project variables

client = automl.AutoMlClient()

project_id = "your_project_id"

location = "us-central1"

dataset_id = "your_dataset_id"

model_display_name = "automl_model"


# Create a client and train a model

response = client.create_model(
    parent=f"projects/{project_id}/locations/{location}",
    model={
        "display_name": model_display_name,
        "dataset_id": dataset_id,
```

"translation_model_metadata": {}, # Modify based on your task type

  },

)

Get the operation status

print("Training   operation   name: {}".format(response.operation.name))

print("Training started...")

6. Automating Retraining with AutoML in MLOps Pipelines

To fully integrate AutoML into MLOps, the AutoML steps can be incorporated into a CI/CD pipeline using tools like Kubeflow Pipelines or MLflow.

Example: Kubeflow Pipeline with AutoML Component (Pseudocode)

```
import kfp

from kfp import dsl


@dsl.pipeline(name="AutoML Pipeline")

def automl_pipeline():

    # Data preprocessing step

    preprocess_op = dsl.ContainerOp(

        name="Preprocess Data",

        image="preprocess-image",

        command=["python", "preprocess.py"],
```

```
    arguments=["--input",        "/data/input",         "--output",
"/data/output"]
  )


  # AutoML training step
  automl_op = dsl.ContainerOp(
    name="AutoML Training",
    image="automl-image",
    command=["python", "automl_train.py"],
    arguments=["--data",   preprocess_op.outputs["output"],   "--
output", "/model/output"]
  )


  # Model deployment step
  deploy_op = dsl.ContainerOp(
    name="Deploy Model",
    image="deploy-image",
    command=["python", "deploy.py"],
    arguments=["--model", automl_op.outputs["output"]]
  )


kfp.compiler.Compiler().compile(automl_pipeline,
"automl_pipeline.yaml")
```

Summary

AutoML integration can significantly reduce model development time by automating crucial steps like model selection,

286

hyperparameter tuning, and pipeline optimization. The choice of framework and pipeline configuration depends on the complexity of your data, desired model performance, and available compute resources.

Handling Multi-Model Deployments

Handling multi-model deployments involves managing multiple machine learning models simultaneously in a production environment. This setup is commonly used in applications that require several models to work in parallel, like recommendation systems, personalization, fraud detection, or multi-tenant systems. Here's a detailed guide on best practices, architecture, and code for deploying and managing multi-model systems.

1. Understanding Multi-Model Deployment Scenarios

- **Multi-Tenancy**: Deploying different models for different users or customer segments.
- **Model Versioning**: Serving multiple versions of the same model, especially in A/B testing or blue-green deployment.
- **Complex Pipelines**: Combining multiple models in a single pipeline for complex tasks (e.g., a sequence of NLP models for text processing).
- **Ensemble Learning**: Deploying ensemble models where predictions from multiple models are combined.

2. Strategies for Multi-Model Deployment

- **Single Model per Endpoint**: Each model is served on a separate endpoint, ideal for simpler deployments but requires more resources.
- **Multi-Model Server**: Deploy multiple models on the same server, which can save resources. The server

dynamically loads and unloads models based on requests.

- **Model Orchestration**: Use an orchestrator like Kubernetes or serverless frameworks to manage scaling and routing across multiple model instances.

3. Multi-Model Deployment Architecture

- **Model Registry**: Maintain a model registry (e.g., MLflow, AWS S3) that stores model versions and metadata.
- **Model Router**: A routing layer directs incoming requests to the appropriate model based on request type, model version, or client requirements.
- **Inference API Layer**: A REST API or gRPC interface that serves predictions. This API manages requests for different models and handles response aggregation when required.
- **Monitoring and Logging**: Continuously monitor model performance, usage, and latency.

4. Multi-Model Deployment with FastAPI and MLflow

Let's walk through a Python-based deployment solution using **FastAPI** for the REST API and **MLflow** for model storage and loading.

Step 1: Model Training and Registration

First, train your models and log them to MLflow.

```python
import mlflow

from sklearn.ensemble import RandomForestClassifier

from sklearn.datasets import load_iris

from sklearn.model_selection import train_test_split


# Train and register multiple models
```

```
data = load_iris()

X_train, X_test, y_train, y_test = train_test_split(data.data,
data.target, test_size=0.2, random_state=42)


for i, max_depth in enumerate([3, 5, 10], start=1):

    model    =    RandomForestClassifier(max_depth=max_depth,
random_state=42)

    model.fit(X_train, y_train)

    with
mlflow.start_run(run_name=f"rf_model_depth_{max_depth}"):

        mlflow.sklearn.log_model(model,
f"model_rf_depth_{max_depth}")
```

Step 2: Build the Model Serving API with FastAPI

Create a FastAPI app to load models dynamically from the MLflow registry and serve predictions. Here, we use a dictionary to manage loaded models, so each model is loaded only once.

```
import mlflow.pyfunc

from fastapi import FastAPI, HTTPException

from pydantic import BaseModel

from typing import List

import numpy as np


app = FastAPI()

model_registry = {}


# Define request schema

class PredictionRequest(BaseModel):
```

```python
    model_name: str

    data: List[List[float]]


@app.on_event("startup")

def load_models():

    # Load all models from MLflow registry into memory

    model_registry['model_rf_depth_3']                    =
mlflow.pyfunc.load_model("models:/model_rf_depth_3/productio
n")

    model_registry['model_rf_depth_5']                    =
mlflow.pyfunc.load_model("models:/model_rf_depth_5/productio
n")

    model_registry['model_rf_depth_10']                   =
mlflow.pyfunc.load_model("models:/model_rf_depth_10/producti
on")

    print("Models loaded")


@app.post("/predict/")

async def predict(request: PredictionRequest):

    model_name = request.model_name

    if model_name not in model_registry:

        raise    HTTPException(status_code=404,    detail=f"Model
{model_name} not found.")


    model = model_registry[model_name]

    data = np.array(request.data)

    predictions = model.predict(data).tolist()
```

return {"predictions": predictions}

Step 3: Run the FastAPI Application

Run the FastAPI app locally to serve predictions.

uvicorn main:app --host 0.0.0.0 --port 8000

Now, you can send requests to specific models by specifying the model name in the request.

Step 4: Sending Prediction Requests

Use curl or any HTTP client to make requests to the models.

```
curl -X POST "http://127.0.0.1:8000/predict/" -H "Content-Type: application/json" -d '{
  "model_name": "model_rf_depth_5",
  "data": [[5.1, 3.5, 1.4, 0.2], [6.2, 3.4, 5.4, 2.3]]
}'
```

Step 5: Model Versioning and Updating

With MLflow, you can update and deploy newer versions of models. You can use a versioning strategy, e.g., update the production tag for the latest model version or add new models as needed.

5. Scaling Multi-Model Deployment with Kubernetes

For larger applications, using Kubernetes can streamline managing multiple models at scale. You can use Kubernetes' Horizontal Pod Autoscaling (HPA) to dynamically scale model services based on CPU/memory or custom metrics (like request load).

1. **Define Kubernetes Deployment for Each Model**

For each model, define a Kubernetes deployment file, model_rf_depth_3_deployment.yaml, for example:

```
apiVersion: apps/v1

kind: Deployment

metadata:

 name: model-rf-depth-3

spec:

 replicas: 2

 selector:

  matchLabels:

   app: model-rf-depth-3

 template:

  metadata:

   labels:

    app: model-rf-depth-3

  spec:

   containers:

   - name: model-rf-depth-3

    image: my-docker-repo/model-rf-depth-3:latest

    ports:

    - containerPort: 8000
```

1. **Configure Load Balancing and Routing**

   Use an API Gateway (like Kong or NGINX) to route requests to the correct model endpoint. Alternatively, create custom routing within your application based on model metadata.

6. Monitoring and Logging for Multi-Model Deployments

Monitoring each model's performance is critical to understanding usage patterns and identifying issues. Common metrics include:

- **Latency**: Measure time taken for inference.
- **Throughput**: Track the number of requests processed.
- **Errors**: Monitor error rates per model.
- **Model Performance**: Use metrics such as accuracy, precision, recall (this may require model re-evaluation on a sample of requests).

Tools for Monitoring:

- **Prometheus and Grafana**: Collect and visualize metrics.
- **ELK Stack (Elasticsearch, Logstash, Kibana)**: Store and analyze logs for insights on errors and performance.

7. Automated Retraining and Model Management

To automate updates, you can integrate MLOps platforms like **Kubeflow**, **MLflow**, or **Tecton** to handle model versioning, drift detection, and retraining workflows.

- **Drift Detection**: Automatically monitor data or concept drift using tools like Alibi Detect. When drift is detected, trigger a retraining workflow.
- **Model Registry Integration**: Update models in your registry and dynamically load new versions without redeploying the entire application.
- **CI/CD Pipeline**: Implement CI/CD for continuous integration and delivery of updated models. Use Docker, GitHub Actions, or Jenkins to automate testing, packaging, and deployment of new model versions.

This multi-model deployment setup allows for flexibility, scalability, and maintainability in production environments, making it suitable for handling high-traffic applications and applications requiring multiple models.

Feature Engineering and Feature Stores

In MLOps (Machine Learning Operations), **Feature Engineering** and **Feature Stores** play vital roles in standardizing data transformations, ensuring feature consistency across different ML models, and streamlining feature reuse across teams. Here's a deep dive into how these components are integrated into an MLOps workflow, along with examples and code implementations.

1. Feature Engineering in MLOps

Feature engineering involves creating new variables or features from raw data, transforming the data to enhance the performance of ML models. This is critical in MLOps, as feature engineering often needs to be consistent across training, validation, and deployment stages to avoid data leakage or performance inconsistencies.

Common Feature Engineering Tasks:

- **Scaling/Normalization**: Standardize or normalize data for better model performance.
- **Encoding**: Convert categorical variables to numerical formats, e.g., one-hot encoding.
- **Feature Selection**: Identify and select the most predictive features.
- **Aggregation**: Aggregate features, such as moving averages or rolling windows, particularly in time series data.
- **Text Vectorization**: Convert text data into vectors for NLP models.

Example: Basic Feature Engineering Pipeline

In a production MLOps pipeline, it's best to encapsulate feature engineering in a reusable function or script to ensure reproducibility. Here's a code snippet using **scikit-learn** and **Pandas** to create a feature engineering pipeline.

```python
import pandas as pd

from sklearn.preprocessing import StandardScaler, OneHotEncoder

from sklearn.compose import ColumnTransformer

from sklearn.pipeline import Pipeline

from sklearn.impute import SimpleImputer

from sklearn.feature_extraction.text import TfidfVectorizer


# Sample data
data = pd.DataFrame({
    'age': [25, 32, 40, 28, None],
    'income': [50000, 60000, 70000, None, 45000],
    'occupation': ['engineer', 'doctor', 'lawyer', 'engineer', 'doctor'],
    'comments': ["great service", "okay", "will not recommend", "good", "excellent"]
})


# Define transformations
numeric_features = ['age', 'income']
numeric_transformer = Pipeline(steps=[
    ('imputer', SimpleImputer(strategy='mean')),
    ('scaler', StandardScaler())
])
```

```python
categorical_features = ['occupation']
categorical_transformer = Pipeline(steps=[
    ('encoder', OneHotEncoder(handle_unknown='ignore'))
])

text_features = ['comments']
text_transformer = Pipeline(steps=[
    ('tfidf', TfidfVectorizer(max_features=5))
])

# Combine transformations
preprocessor = ColumnTransformer(
    transformers=[
        ('num', numeric_transformer, numeric_features),
        ('cat', categorical_transformer, categorical_features),
        ('text', 'passthrough', text_features)  # Text transformer
    ]
)

# Transform the data
data_transformed = preprocessor.fit_transform(data)
print(data_transformed)
```

2. Feature Stores in MLOps

Feature stores provide a centralized repository to store, manage, and serve features for machine learning. This allows teams to:

- Reuse features across different ML models and projects.
- Serve consistent features during training and production to prevent training-serving skew.
- Track feature versions and metadata for auditing and lineage.
- Automatically update real-time features with streaming data.

Types of Feature Stores:

- **Batch Feature Store**: Primarily for historical data used in model training.
- **Real-Time Feature Store**: Supports low-latency feature serving for online predictions.

Popular Feature Store Tools:

- **Feast** (Feature Store for Machine Learning)
- **Tecton**
- **Amazon SageMaker Feature Store**
- **Databricks Feature Store**

3. Implementing a Feature Store with Feast

Feast (Feature Store) is a popular open-source feature store that integrates with MLOps pipelines. Feast can ingest features from batch or streaming sources, store them in databases, and serve them in production.

Step 1: Setting Up Feast

Install Feast and necessary dependencies:

pip install feast

Step 2: Define Feature Definitions in Feast

Define feature sets by describing the entities (e.g., customer_id) and feature transformations. Here's an example configuration for user-related features:

```python
from feast import Entity, Feature, FeatureView, ValueType

from feast.data_format import ParquetFormat

from feast.infra.offline_stores.file_source import FileSource


# Define entity for customer

customer = Entity(name="customer_id", value_type=ValueType.INT64, description="Customer ID")


# Define data source

user_data = FileSource(
    path="data/user_data.parquet",  # Example data source
    event_timestamp_column="event_timestamp",
    created_timestamp_column="created_timestamp"
)


# Define feature view

user_features = FeatureView(
    name="user_features",
    entities=["customer_id"],
    ttl=timedelta(days=1),
    features=[
```

```
    Feature(name="age", dtype=ValueType.INT64),

    Feature(name="income", dtype=ValueType.FLOAT),

    Feature(name="signup_date", dtype=ValueType.STRING)

  ],

  batch_source=user_data,

)
```

Step 3: Materialize and Retrieve Features with Feast

Materialization in Feast syncs offline and online features, enabling real-time model serving.

```
from datetime import datetime

from feast import FeatureStore


# Initialize feature store

store = FeatureStore(repo_path="path/to/feature_repo")


# Materialize features into online store (real-time availability)

store.materialize(start_date=datetime(2023,        1,        1),
end_date=datetime(2023, 12, 31))


# Retrieve feature vector for a given customer

entity_df = pd.DataFrame.from_dict({"customer_id": [123]})

feature_vector = store.get_online_features(

    features=["user_features:age", "user_features:income"],

    entity_rows=entity_df.to_dict("records")

).to_df()
```

```
print(feature_vector)
```

4. Feature Engineering Pipelines and Feature Store Integration in MLOps

In MLOps, feature stores can be integrated into feature engineering pipelines using tools like **Kubeflow Pipelines** or **Apache Airflow**. This integration enables feature engineering to be part of the model CI/CD, making it reproducible, trackable, and automatable.

Example: Using Airflow with Feast

With Airflow, we can schedule daily updates to the feature store and automate materialization jobs.

```
from airflow import DAG

from airflow.operators.python_operator import PythonOperator

from datetime import datetime, timedelta

from feast import FeatureStore


# Define DAG and schedule

default_args = {"owner": "airflow", "retries": 1, "retry_delay": timedelta(minutes=5)}

dag = DAG("feature_store_materialization", default_args=default_args, start_date=datetime(2023, 1, 1), schedule_interval="@daily")


# Define materialization task

def materialize_features():

    store = FeatureStore(repo_path="path/to/feature_repo")
```

```
store.materialize(start_date=datetime.now()        -
timedelta(days=1), end_date=datetime.now())


materialize_task                                   =
PythonOperator(task_id="materialize_features",
python_callable=materialize_features, dag=dag)


# Set up Airflow DAG

materialize_task
```

5. Benefits of Feature Engineering and Feature Stores in MLOps

- **Reusability**: Feature stores allow teams to reuse features across projects and models, saving time and reducing duplication.
- **Consistency**: Features are defined once and remain consistent across training and production, reducing training-serving skew.
- **Automation**: Automated feature pipelines enable data ingestion, transformation, and real-time serving, critical in large-scale applications.
- **Monitoring and Governance**: Feature stores enable tracking of feature lineage, versioning, and metadata, aiding governance, and compliance.

Summary

Feature engineering and feature stores are key components in MLOps. Feature engineering creates optimized features for models, while feature stores ensure consistency and availability of these features across different environments. Together, they support scalable, reusable, and reliable ML pipelines.

Real-time Model Inference and Streaming

In MLOps, **Real-time Model Inference** and **Streaming** allow for instantaneous model predictions on live data, supporting applications such as recommendation engines, fraud detection, and dynamic pricing. Real-time inference processes incoming data in milliseconds to seconds, while streaming enables continuous data processing, ensuring that models make predictions on new data immediately as it arrives.

Here's a detailed overview of real-time inference and streaming in MLOps, along with code to set up an example.

1. Real-Time Model Inference

Real-time model inference involves serving ML models with minimal latency to provide predictions as quickly as possible. In MLOps, real-time inference pipelines typically consist of:

- **Model Serving Infrastructure**: Deploying models to scalable serving platforms, such as **FastAPI, Flask, TensorFlow Serving**, or cloud-based solutions like **AWS SageMaker, Azure ML**, or **Google AI Platform**.
- **Request and Response Optimization**: Using optimized data formats (e.g., Protobuf or JSON) and ensuring efficient data serialization.
- **Monitoring and Logging**: Tracking latency, throughput, and error rates to maintain the quality of predictions.

Example: Setting Up Real-Time Inference with FastAPI and Redis for Caching

In this example, we use **FastAPI** to deploy the model and **Redis** as an in-memory store for caching recent predictions, reducing latency and improving scalability.

Step 1: Train and Save the Model

```python
import joblib

from sklearn.datasets import load_iris

from sklearn.ensemble import RandomForestClassifier


# Train a simple model

data = load_iris()

X, y = data.data, data.target

model = RandomForestClassifier()

model.fit(X, y)


# Save the model

joblib.dump(model, 'iris_model.joblib')
```

Step 2: Serve the Model with FastAPI

Install dependencies:

```
pip install fastapi uvicorn redis joblib
```

Set up the FastAPI app for real-time inference. The API will load the model, receive incoming data, and return predictions.

```python
from fastapi import FastAPI, HTTPException

from pydantic import BaseModel

import numpy as np

import joblib

import redis


# Initialize FastAPI app and Redis client
```

```python
app = FastAPI()
cache = redis.Redis(host='localhost', port=6379, db=0)

# Load the model
model = joblib.load('iris_model.joblib')

# Define request schema
class InferenceRequest(BaseModel):
    data: list

@app.post("/predict")
async def predict(request: InferenceRequest):
    # Convert data to numpy array
    data_array = np.array(request.data)

    # Check cache
    cache_key = str(data_array.tobytes())
    cached_result = cache.get(cache_key)

    if cached_result:
        # Return cached prediction if available
        return {"predictions": cached_result.decode("utf-8")}

    # Make prediction
    prediction = model.predict(data_array.reshape(1, -1)).tolist()
```

```
# Store result in cache

cache.set(cache_key, str(prediction))


return {"predictions": prediction}
```

Run the FastAPI app:

```
uvicorn main:app --host 0.0.0.0 --port 8000
```

Step 3: Test the Real-Time Inference

You can now test the API with a POST request using **curl** or any HTTP client.

```
curl -X POST "http://127.0.0.1:8000/predict" -H "Content-Type: application/json" -d '{"data": [5.1, 3.5, 1.4, 0.2]}'
```

2. Streaming Data Processing

Streaming in MLOps involves continuous processing and handling of real-time data as it arrives, which is critical for updating model predictions or features in real-time. **Apache Kafka** and **Apache Spark Structured Streaming** are widely used for managing and processing streaming data in MLOps.

Example: Real-Time Model Inference with Kafka and Spark Structured Streaming

In this example, Kafka will serve as the message broker to handle data streams, while Spark Structured Streaming will process the data and apply the ML model in real-time.

Step 1: Set Up Kafka Producer to Stream Data

1. Install Kafka and start the Kafka server.
2. Write a producer to send messages to a Kafka topic.

```python
from kafka import KafkaProducer

import json

import numpy as np

import time


# Create Kafka producer

producer = KafkaProducer(bootstrap_servers='localhost:9092',
value_serializer=lambda v: json.dumps(v).encode('utf-8'))


# Send data to Kafka topic 'real-time-data'

while True:

    # Generate synthetic data

    data = np.random.rand(4).tolist()

    producer.send('real-time-data', {'data': data})

    time.sleep(1)  # Send data every second
```

Step 2: Set Up Spark Structured Streaming for Model Inference

Now, set up a **Spark Structured Streaming** job to consume data from Kafka, apply the model, and output the predictions to another Kafka topic.

```python
from pyspark.sql import SparkSession

from pyspark.ml.classification import RandomForestClassifierModel

from pyspark.ml.linalg import Vectors

from pyspark.sql.functions import udf, col

from pyspark.sql.types import ArrayType, FloatType, IntegerType
```

```python
# Initialize Spark session
spark = SparkSession.builder.appName("RealTimeModelInference").getOrCreate()


# Load pre-trained Spark ML model (Assuming model is saved in Spark ML format)
model = RandomForestClassifierModel.load("path_to_spark_model")


# Define UDF for model prediction
@udf(returnType=IntegerType())
def predict(data):
    vector = Vectors.dense(data)
    prediction = model.predict(vector)
    return prediction


# Read data from Kafka
streaming_df = spark \
    .readStream \
    .format("kafka") \
    .option("kafka.bootstrap.servers", "localhost:9092") \
    .option("subscribe", "real-time-data") \
    .load()
```

```
# Convert Kafka value to String and parse JSON

streaming_df = streaming_df.selectExpr("CAST(value AS
STRING) as json")

parsed_df = streaming_df.selectExpr("json_extract(json, '$.data')
AS data")


# Apply the prediction UDF

predictions_df = parsed_df.withColumn("prediction",
predict(col("data")))


# Write predictions to a Kafka topic

query = predictions_df \
    .selectExpr("CAST(prediction AS STRING) AS value") \
    .writeStream \
    .format("kafka") \
    .option("kafka.bootstrap.servers", "localhost:9092") \
    .option("topic", "predictions") \
    .option("checkpointLocation", "/tmp/checkpoints") \
    .start()


query.awaitTermination()
```

3. Integration of Real-Time Inference with Feature Stores

In production MLOps systems, real-time inference often integrates with feature stores to access real-time or historical features. For example:

- **Retrieve features** from a feature store such as Feast just before inference to ensure the latest feature values.
- **Real-time updates** to the feature store based on new incoming data, providing consistent feature availability across multiple models.

4. Monitoring Real-Time Inference and Streaming

Monitoring real-time pipelines is critical for reliability. Common metrics to track include:

- **Latency**: Time taken to serve each request.
- **Throughput**: Number of requests per second or minute.
- **Error rates**: Track errors to monitor system health.
- **Data Drift Detection**: Identify shifts in input data distribution that could affect model performance.

Tools for Monitoring:

- **Prometheus** and **Grafana** for monitoring and visualization.
- **ELK Stack (Elasticsearch, Logstash, Kibana)** for logging and real-time analysis.
- **Alibi Detect** for monitoring data drift and model performance.

Summary

Real-time model inference and streaming are critical components in MLOps for applications that require fast, low-latency predictions. By using tools like FastAPI for model serving, Kafka for message streaming, and Spark Structured Streaming for data processing, you can build scalable, real-time ML pipelines. Integrating with a feature store further ensures that real-time models have consistent, up-to-date features for making accurate predictions. Monitoring these systems provides reliability and transparency in production.

Chapter-14 Case Studies in MLOps

MLOps in Finance: Fraud Detection

In finance, **fraud detection** is a critical application for MLOps (Machine Learning Operations). Using MLOps principles for fraud detection allows financial institutions to detect suspicious activities in real-time or near real-time, leveraging machine learning models that can scale, adapt to new threats, and integrate seamlessly into operational systems.

This overview includes steps to build and deploy a fraud detection system with MLOps principles, covering feature engineering, model training, deployment, monitoring, and code examples.

1. Problem Overview: Fraud Detection in Finance

Fraud detection models aim to classify transactions as either **fraudulent** or **non-fraudulent**. Key steps in building a fraud detection system include:

- **Data Collection and Labeling**: Collect historical transaction data, labeled as fraudulent or non-fraudulent.

- **Data Preprocessing**: Clean and preprocess data, including handling missing values, normalizing features, and encoding categorical variables.
- **Feature Engineering**: Generate meaningful features that help identify fraud patterns, such as transaction amount, time between transactions, or customer-specific spending habits.
- **Model Training**: Train a machine learning model (e.g., logistic regression, random forest, or XGBoost) to classify transactions.
- **Real-Time Deployment**: Deploy the model using an API for real-time fraud detection.
- **Monitoring and Updating**: Continuously monitor model performance and update it when necessary to ensure it adapts to new fraud patterns.

2. Data Preprocessing and Feature Engineering

Fraud detection typically uses features like transaction amount, transaction time, location, device, and customer transaction history.

Example Code: Data Preprocessing and Feature Engineering

For this example, we'll assume we have a sample dataset with features like transaction_amount, transaction_time, location, and device_type.

```
import pandas as pd

import numpy as np

from sklearn.preprocessing import StandardScaler, LabelEncoder

from datetime import datetime


# Sample data

data = pd.DataFrame({
```

```
    'transaction_amount': [100.0, 250.5, 450.7, 30.5, 600.0],

    'transaction_time':    ['2023-10-10    12:05:30',    '2023-10-11
08:30:45',

                    '2023-10-11  17:05:10', '2023-10-12  14:30:20',
'2023-10-13 10:05:25'],

    'location': ['NY', 'CA', 'CA', 'TX', 'NY'],

    'device_type': ['mobile', 'desktop', 'desktop', 'mobile', 'tablet'],

    'is_fraud': [0, 1, 0, 0, 1]

})


# Convert transaction_time to datetime and extract features

data['transaction_time']                                           =
pd.to_datetime(data['transaction_time'])

data['hour'] = data['transaction_time'].dt.hour

data['day_of_week'] = data['transaction_time'].dt.dayofweek


# Encode categorical features

label_encoder = LabelEncoder()

data['location_encoded']                                           =
label_encoder.fit_transform(data['location'])

data['device_type_encoded']                                        =
label_encoder.fit_transform(data['device_type'])


# Scale numerical features

scaler = StandardScaler()

data['transaction_amount_scaled']                                  =
scaler.fit_transform(data[['transaction_amount']])
```

```
# Features for the model
```

features = data[['transaction_amount_scaled', 'hour', 'day_of_week', 'location_encoded', 'device_type_encoded']]

labels = data['is_fraud']

print(features.head())

3. Model Training

Fraud detection models are often binary classifiers. Here we'll use **Random Forest** as an example model, which is effective for classification tasks with imbalanced data.

from sklearn.ensemble import RandomForestClassifier

from sklearn.model_selection import train_test_split

from sklearn.metrics import classification_report, accuracy_score

```
# Split data into training and testing sets
```

X_train, X_test, y_train, y_test = train_test_split(features, labels, test_size=0.2, random_state=42)

```
# Train the model
```

model = RandomForestClassifier(n_estimators=100, random_state=42)

model.fit(X_train, y_train)

```
# Evaluate the model
```

y_pred = model.predict(X_test)

```
print("Accuracy:", accuracy_score(y_test, y_pred))
```

```
print(classification_report(y_test, y_pred))
```

4. Model Deployment with FastAPI

To deploy the model, we use **FastAPI** to create an API that receives transaction data and returns fraud predictions. This API will be part of a real-time fraud detection system in production.

Install Dependencies
```
pip install fastapi uvicorn joblib
```

Save the Model

```
import joblib
```

```
joblib.dump(model, 'fraud_detection_model.joblib')
```

Create FastAPI App

```
from fastapi import FastAPI
```

```
from pydantic import BaseModel
```

```
import joblib
```

```
import numpy as np
```

```
# Load the model
```

```
model = joblib.load('fraud_detection_model.joblib')
```

```
# Initialize FastAPI app
```

```
app = FastAPI()
```

```
# Define input schema
```

```
class Transaction(BaseModel):
```

```
    transaction_amount: float

    transaction_time: str  # 'YYYY-MM-DD HH:MM:SS'

    location: str

    device_type: str


@app.post("/predict")

async def predict(transaction: Transaction):

    # Extract and preprocess data

    transaction_time                                    =
    datetime.strptime(transaction.transaction_time,     "%Y-%m-%d
    %H:%M:%S")

    hour = transaction_time.hour

    day_of_week = transaction_time.weekday()


    location_encoded                                    =
    label_encoder.transform([transaction.location])[0]

    device_type_encoded                                 =
    label_encoder.transform([transaction.device_type])[0]


    transaction_amount_scaled                           =
    scaler.transform([[transaction.transaction_amount]])[0][0]


    # Prepare features for prediction

    features    =    np.array([[transaction_amount_scaled,    hour,
    day_of_week, location_encoded, device_type_encoded]])


    # Get prediction
```

```
prediction = model.predict(features)[0]
```

```
# Return result
return {"is_fraud": bool(prediction)}
```

Run the API:

```
uvicorn main:app --host 0.0.0.0 --port 8000
```

Test the API

```
curl -X POST "http://127.0.0.1:8000/predict" -H "Content-Type:
application/json" -d '{

  "transaction_amount": 300.5,

  "transaction_time": "2023-10-12 10:00:00",

  "location": "NY",

  "device_type": "mobile"

}'
```

5. Monitoring and Alerting

Continuous monitoring is essential in fraud detection to ensure the model performs reliably and detects new patterns of fraudulent activities.

- **Latency Monitoring**: Track response times of model predictions.
- **Accuracy and Drift Detection**: Regularly evaluate model accuracy. Use tools like **Alibi Detect** to identify data or concept drift, indicating that the model might need retraining.
- **Logging and Alerting**: Integrate with logging services (e.g., **ELK Stack** or **Prometheus/Grafana**) to log errors, unusual activity, and monitor resource utilization.

6. Automating the Pipeline with CI/CD

Automating the entire fraud detection workflow is important for quick adaptation to changing fraud patterns. Using CI/CD practices, such as **GitHub Actions** or **Jenkins**, can automate model retraining, testing, and deployment.

Example CI/CD Workflow:

- **Step 1**: Retrain the model with new data periodically or on detecting drift.
- **Step 2**: Run tests to validate model performance.
- **Step 3**: Deploy the model to the production API if it meets performance thresholds.
- **Step 4**: Monitor the model in production and trigger alerts if performance degrades.

Summary

MLOps for fraud detection in finance combines machine learning, feature engineering, model deployment, and continuous monitoring. By using tools such as FastAPI for deployment and CI/CD pipelines for automation, MLOps ensures the fraud detection model remains effective and responsive to new threats. Continuous monitoring and drift detection keep the model updated, providing robust defense against fraud in dynamic financial environments.

MLOps in Healthcare: Predictive Analytics

In healthcare, **MLOps for Predictive Analytics** enables organizations to leverage machine learning to predict patient outcomes, optimize resources, and improve care delivery. Implementing predictive analytics in healthcare involves using patient data (e.g., demographics, medical history, and lab results) to predict events like hospital readmission, disease risk, or treatment outcomes. MLOps practices help manage the deployment, monitoring, and continuous improvement of these models.

Here's a detailed guide to implementing MLOps for predictive analytics in healthcare, including the workflow, model building, deployment, and monitoring.

1. Problem Overview: Predictive Analytics in Healthcare

In this example, we'll focus on **predicting hospital readmission** within 30 days, which is a common healthcare use case. Reducing readmission rates can improve patient outcomes and reduce costs for healthcare providers.

Key steps in developing a predictive analytics solution include:

- **Data Collection and Preprocessing**: Collect and preprocess data such as patient demographics, lab results, medications, and previous admissions.
- **Feature Engineering**: Generate features that capture patient health status and healthcare utilization patterns.
- **Model Training**: Train a model to predict readmission risk.
- **Model Deployment**: Deploy the model using an API for real-time or batch predictions.
- **Monitoring and Updating**: Continuously monitor the model's performance and update it to adapt to new trends in patient data.

2. Data Preprocessing and Feature Engineering

In healthcare, preprocessing includes handling missing values, standardizing lab values, encoding categorical variables, and generating useful features based on medical history.

Example Code: Data Preprocessing and Feature Engineering

For this example, let's assume we have a dataset with columns like age, gender, lab_results, previous_admissions, and readmitted (the target variable).

```python
import pandas as pd

from sklearn.preprocessing import StandardScaler, LabelEncoder

from sklearn.model_selection import train_test_split


# Sample data

data = pd.DataFrame({

    'age': [45, 70, 50, 80, 65],

    'gender': ['female', 'male', 'female', 'male', 'female'],

    'lab_results': [120, 130, 110, 125, 115],

    'previous_admissions': [2, 5, 1, 4, 3],

    'readmitted': [1, 0, 1, 0, 1]

})


# Encode categorical features

label_encoder = LabelEncoder()

data['gender_encoded'] = label_encoder.fit_transform(data['gender'])
```

```python
# Scale numerical features

scaler = StandardScaler()

data['age_scaled'] = scaler.fit_transform(data[['age']])

data['lab_results_scaled']                              =
scaler.fit_transform(data[['lab_results']])
```

```python
# Features and target

features      =      data[['age_scaled',      'gender_encoded',
'lab_results_scaled', 'previous_admissions']]

labels = data['readmitted']
```

```python
print(features.head())
```

3. Model Training

We'll use a **logistic regression** model for this example to predict
the probability of readmission within 30 days. Logistic regression
is a good starting point for binary classification problems and can
be deployed easily.

```python
from sklearn.linear_model import LogisticRegression

from sklearn.metrics import accuracy_score, classification_report
```

```python
# Split the dataset

X_train, X_test, y_train, y_test = train_test_split(features, labels,
test_size=0.2, random_state=42)
```

```
# Train the model

model = LogisticRegression()

model.fit(X_train, y_train)


# Evaluate the model

y_pred = model.predict(X_test)

print("Accuracy:", accuracy_score(y_test, y_pred))

print(classification_report(y_test, y_pred))
```

4. Model Deployment with FastAPI

Once the model is trained, we can deploy it using FastAPI to create an API that predicts readmission probability based on patient data. This API could be integrated into electronic health record (EHR) systems for real-time predictions.

Install Dependencies

```
pip install fastapi uvicorn joblib
```

Save the Model

```
import joblib

joblib.dump(model, 'readmission_model.joblib')
```

Create FastAPI App

```
from fastapi import FastAPI
```

```python
from pydantic import BaseModel

import joblib

import numpy as np


# Load the model

model = joblib.load('readmission_model.joblib')


# Initialize FastAPI app

app = FastAPI()


# Define input schema

class PatientData(BaseModel):

    age: float

    gender: str

    lab_results: float

    previous_admissions: int


@app.post("/predict")

async def predict(data: PatientData):

    # Preprocess input data
```

```python
age_scaled = scaler.transform([[data.age]])[0][0]

lab_results_scaled = scaler.transform([[data.lab_results]])[0][0]

gender_encoded = label_encoder.transform([data.gender])[0]


# Prepare features for prediction

features = np.array([[age_scaled, gender_encoded, lab_results_scaled, data.previous_admissions]])


# Get prediction

prediction = model.predict(features)[0]

probability = model.predict_proba(features)[0][1]


# Return result

return {"readmission": bool(prediction), "probability": probability}
```

Run the API:

```
uvicorn main:app --host 0.0.0.0 --port 8000
```

Test the API

You can test the API using curl or a tool like Postman.

```
curl -X POST "http://127.0.0.1:8000/predict" -H "Content-Type: application/json" -d '{
```

"age": 65,

"gender": "female",

"lab_results": 115,

"previous_admissions": 3

}'

5. Monitoring and Alerting

Monitoring is crucial for healthcare models to ensure reliable performance over time and detect data drift. Common metrics include:

- **Prediction Accuracy**: Track the model's accuracy over time.
- **Data Drift Detection**: Use tools like **Alibi Detect** to monitor changes in input data distribution.
- **Latency Monitoring**: Track response times to maintain low latency, especially for real-time predictions.

Monitoring Tools:

- **Prometheus/Grafana** for monitoring and visualizing API latency, request counts, and errors.
- **ELK Stack (Elasticsearch, Logstash, Kibana)** for logging and tracking anomalies.
- **Alibi Detect** for data drift detection, ensuring that the model adapts to changes in healthcare data over time.

6. Automating the Pipeline with CI/CD

A CI/CD pipeline is essential to automate the retraining and redeployment process for healthcare models, especially when patient data evolves. With **CI/CD**, you can automatically retrain, test, and deploy models whenever there are updates to patient data or new features added.

Example CI/CD Workflow:

1. **Data Update**: Collect new patient data periodically or in batches.
2. **Model Retraining**: Retrain the model with the latest data when performance metrics (like accuracy or AUC) fall below a threshold.
3. **Automated Testing**: Run automated tests to validate the model's performance.
4. **Deployment**: Deploy the updated model automatically to the FastAPI server.
5. **Monitoring and Logging**: Set up continuous monitoring for real-time performance tracking.

Example CI/CD Tools:

- **GitHub Actions** or **Jenkins** for automating the build and deployment pipeline.
- **Docker** to containerize the API and deploy it consistently across environments.
- **Kubernetes** for scalable deployment and orchestration in healthcare systems.

Summary

Predictive analytics in healthcare, supported by MLOps practices, helps healthcare providers manage patient risks and improve outcomes. By implementing a robust MLOps pipeline with automated preprocessing, real-time model deployment using FastAPI, and CI/CD for continuous model updates, healthcare organizations can deploy predictive models that adapt to evolving data. This system includes data drift detection, accuracy monitoring, and response-time tracking, ensuring that models in production perform reliably and can respond to new trends in patient health data.

MLOps in Retail: Demand Forecasting

In retail, **MLOps for Demand Forecasting** allows businesses to anticipate demand for products more accurately, helping with inventory management, reducing stockouts, and optimizing supply chains. MLOps principles support the continuous deployment, monitoring, and retraining of demand forecasting models to adapt to changing market conditions, seasonal variations, and customer preferences.

Here's a detailed guide to implementing MLOps for demand forecasting in retail, covering data preprocessing, model training, deployment, and monitoring.

1. Problem Overview: Demand Forecasting in Retail

The goal of demand forecasting is to predict future demand for products based on historical sales data, promotions, holidays, and other factors. Key steps in a demand forecasting workflow include:

- **Data Collection and Preprocessing**: Collect historical sales data, external factors (e.g., promotions, holidays), and preprocess it.
- **Feature Engineering**: Generate features that represent seasonal patterns, trends, and cyclic behavior in demand.
- **Model Training**: Train time-series forecasting models to predict future demand.
- **Model Deployment**: Deploy the model using an API for real-time or batch demand predictions.
- **Monitoring and Updating**: Continuously monitor model performance and retrain periodically or based on detected data drift.

2. Data Preprocessing and Feature Engineering

In demand forecasting, preprocessing involves handling missing values, creating time-based features, and transforming external factors into meaningful features.

Example Code: Data Preprocessing and Feature Engineering

Assuming we have a dataset with columns such as date, sales, promotion, and holiday, let's create time-based features (e.g., day of the week, month, and is_weekend) and preprocess the data.

```python
import pandas as pd

import numpy as np

from sklearn.preprocessing import StandardScaler

from datetime import datetime


# Sample data
data = pd.DataFrame({

    'date': pd.date_range(start='2023-01-01', periods=100),

    'sales': np.random.randint(50, 200, size=100),

    'promotion': np.random.choice([0, 1], size=100),

    'holiday': np.random.choice([0, 1], size=100)
})


# Create time-based features
data['day_of_week'] = data['date'].dt.dayofweek
data['month'] = data['date'].dt.month
```

```
data['is_weekend'] = data['day_of_week'].apply(lambda x: 1 if x
>= 5 else 0)
```

```
# Scale sales data for model training
```

```
scaler = StandardScaler()
```

```
data['sales_scaled'] = scaler.fit_transform(data[['sales']])
```

```
# Features and target
```

```
features    =    data[['day_of_week',    'month',    'is_weekend',
'promotion', 'holiday']]
```

```
labels = data['sales_scaled']
```

```
print(features.head())
```

3. Model Training

We'll use **XGBoost**, a popular algorithm for time-series forecasting, which works well for structured tabular data and can handle non-linear relationships.

Train-Test Split

To simulate real-world scenarios, we'll split the data into a training set (80%) and a test set (20%).

```
from xgboost import XGBRegressor
```

```
from sklearn.metrics import mean_squared_error
```

```
from sklearn.model_selection import train_test_split
```

```
# Split the dataset
```

```
X_train, X_test, y_train, y_test = train_test_split(features, labels,
test_size=0.2, shuffle=False)
```

```
# Train the model
```

```
model    =    XGBRegressor(n_estimators=100,    max_depth=5,
learning_rate=0.1, random_state=42)
```

```
model.fit(X_train, y_train)
```

```
# Evaluate the model
```

```
y_pred = model.predict(X_test)
```

```
mse = mean_squared_error(y_test, y_pred)
```

```
print("Mean Squared Error:", mse)
```

4. Model Deployment with FastAPI

To deploy the model, we'll use **FastAPI** to create an API for predicting demand. This API can be integrated into inventory management systems for real-time demand forecasting.

Install Dependencies

```
pip install fastapi uvicorn joblib
```

Save the Model

```
import joblib
```

```
joblib.dump(model, 'demand_forecast_model.joblib')
```

Create FastAPI App

```
from fastapi import FastAPI
```

```python
from pydantic import BaseModel

import joblib

import numpy as np


# Load the model

model = joblib.load('demand_forecast_model.joblib')


# Initialize FastAPI app

app = FastAPI()


# Define input schema

class DemandData(BaseModel):

    day_of_week: int

    month: int

    is_weekend: int

    promotion: int

    holiday: int


@app.post("/predict")

async def predict(data: DemandData):
```

```
# Prepare input data for prediction

features    =    np.array([[data.day_of_week,    data.month,
data.is_weekend, data.promotion, data.holiday]])


# Get prediction

prediction = model.predict(features)[0]


# Return result

return {"predicted_sales": float(prediction)}
```

Run the API:

```
uvicorn main:app --host 0.0.0.0 --port 8000
```

Test the API

Test the API by sending a POST request with the input features.

```
curl -X POST "http://127.0.0.1:8000/predict" -H "Content-Type:
application/json" -d '{

  "day_of_week": 3,

  "month": 7,

  "is_weekend": 0,

  "promotion": 1,

  "holiday": 0

}'
```

5. Monitoring and Alerting

Continuous monitoring is essential for demand forecasting models, especially in retail where seasonality and trends can quickly shift. Monitoring strategies include:

- **Accuracy Monitoring**: Regularly track metrics like **Mean Squared Error (MSE)** or **Mean Absolute Percentage Error (MAPE)** on recent predictions to detect performance degradation.
- **Data Drift Detection**: Use tools like **Evidently** or **Alibi Detect** to monitor changes in input data distribution, which could indicate model drift.
- **Latency Monitoring**: Track API response times to ensure real-time predictions are served promptly.

Example Monitoring Tools:

- **Prometheus/Grafana**: For tracking response times, error rates, and request counts.
- **ELK Stack (Elasticsearch, Logstash, Kibana)**: For logging and anomaly detection.
- **Alibi Detect**: For data drift and concept drift detection.

6. Automating the Pipeline with CI/CD

Using CI/CD pipelines, you can automate retraining, testing, and deployment of demand forecasting models. CI/CD pipelines help update the model frequently as new data arrives or when model performance drops.

Example CI/CD Workflow:

1. **Data Ingestion**: Pull new data (e.g., daily sales) into a data warehouse.
2. **Model Retraining**: Set a trigger to retrain the model when new data is available or if performance metrics fall below a threshold.
3. **Automated Testing**: Run tests to ensure the model's predictions meet accuracy standards.

4. **Deployment**: Deploy the updated model automatically to the FastAPI server.
5. **Monitoring**: Set up continuous monitoring for production model performance and alerts for drift.

Tools:

- **GitHub Actions** or **Jenkins** for automating training, testing, and deployment.
- **Docker** to containerize the application for consistency across environments.
- **Kubernetes** for scalable deployment, allowing the API to handle increased demand.

Summary

MLOps for demand forecasting in retail provides a framework for continuously deploying and monitoring models that adapt to changing market trends and customer demands. By implementing a robust MLOps pipeline, retailers can ensure their demand forecasting models remain accurate, scalable, and responsive to real-world changes. This setup includes time-series preprocessing, XGBoost model training, FastAPI deployment, CI/CD pipelines, and monitoring, offering a complete solution to optimize inventory management and reduce costs.

Chapter-15 Future of MLOps

Emerging Trends in MLOps

Emerging trends in **MLOps** (Machine Learning Operations) are transforming how organizations develop, deploy, and maintain machine learning (ML) models. These advancements focus on improving efficiency, scalability, and adaptability, enabling businesses to build more robust AI systems that can respond to real-world changes seamlessly. Here's a look at some of the key trends shaping the future of MLOps:

1. Automated and Continuous Machine Learning (AutoML and CML)

AutoML automates the model-building process, making it easier to experiment with and optimize ML models without deep technical expertise. When combined with **Continuous Machine Learning (CML)**, models can automatically adapt to changing data and evolve over time. This trend is critical as it reduces the need for human intervention in retraining and improves model accuracy without frequent manual updates.

- **Example**: AutoML frameworks like Google's AutoML, H2O.ai, and AutoKeras automate hyperparameter tuning, feature engineering, and model selection.
- **Benefits**: Reduces time to production, lowers barriers to entry, and ensures that models stay updated and optimized over time.

Husn Ara

2. Data-Centric MLOps

Traditional MLOps focuses on model development and infrastructure, but the **data-centric MLOps** approach emphasizes the importance of high-quality data to improve model performance. This trend involves creating robust data pipelines, applying data versioning, and automating data validation to ensure reliable, accurate inputs for ML models.

- **Example**: Tools like **Great Expectations** and **Tecton** facilitate data validation, labeling, and feature engineering, helping to maintain clean, high-quality data for models.
- **Benefits**: Data-centric MLOps leads to better model accuracy, reduced risk of data drift, and more robust ML pipelines.

3. Federated Learning and Privacy-Preserving MLOps

Federated Learning (FL) enables the training of ML models across decentralized devices while keeping data on the devices themselves, preserving privacy and security. With growing concerns around data privacy, federated learning allows organizations to build models without directly accessing sensitive data.

- **Example**: Google's Federated Learning and frameworks like **PySyft** allow data scientists to train models on user data without transferring it to a centralized server.
- **Benefits**: Improves data privacy, reduces legal compliance challenges, and makes ML accessible to industries with sensitive data (e.g., healthcare, finance).

4. Explainable and Responsible AI

As ML models impact critical decisions, **Explainable AI (XAI)** is becoming essential. MLOps frameworks are increasingly incorporating explainability and interpretability tools that help practitioners and stakeholders understand how models make decisions. This transparency also helps meet regulatory requirements and build trust.

335

- **Example**: Tools like **SHAP**, **LIME**, and **Alibi** provide insights into model predictions, making it easier for teams to debug, interpret, and explain model outcomes.
- **Benefits**: Fosters responsible AI practices, improves trust, and ensures compliance with transparency-focused regulations like GDPR.

5. Unified MLOps Platforms

Companies are shifting from using multiple, isolated tools to adopting **unified MLOps platforms** that integrate every stage of the ML lifecycle. Unified platforms provide end-to-end solutions for data ingestion, model training, deployment, monitoring, and version control in a single interface, allowing better collaboration between teams and reducing pipeline complexity.

- **Example**: Platforms like **Databricks**, **Vertex AI** by Google, and **AWS SageMaker** offer integrated MLOps solutions, bringing data engineers, data scientists, and ML engineers together.
- **Benefits**: Streamlines workflows, reduces deployment time, and enhances collaboration.

6. Real-Time Model Inference and Streaming Data

With increased demand for real-time insights, **real-time model inference** is becoming more popular. Organizations are focusing on deploying models that can process streaming data and provide instant predictions. This trend is especially relevant for industries where timely decision-making is crucial, such as finance, e-commerce, and IoT.

- **Example**: **Kafka** and **Apache Flink** are commonly used for real-time data ingestion and processing, enabling ML models to run inference in near real-time.
- **Benefits**: Enables real-time decision-making, improves customer experience, and supports applications requiring rapid responses.

7. ModelOps for Multi-Model and Multi-Cloud Deployments

Organizations are deploying multiple models simultaneously and increasingly using **multi-cloud environments** to avoid vendor lock-in and enhance resilience. **ModelOps** provides centralized management for multi-model and multi-cloud deployments, allowing organizations to monitor, update, and maintain a large number of models across cloud platforms.

- **Example**: Tools like **KubeFlow** and **MLflow** can support model management across clouds (e.g., AWS, Azure, GCP), helping with version control and monitoring across hybrid infrastructures.
- **Benefits**: Enhances scalability, ensures availability, and supports complex ML architectures.

8. Continuous Monitoring and Drift Detection

The demand for **continuous model monitoring** and **drift detection** is growing, as models in production can become less effective due to data drift, concept drift, or changing real-world conditions. Tools are emerging that allow organizations to automatically detect drift and alert teams, helping them retrain or update models as needed.

- **Example**: Libraries like **Evidently** and **WhyLabs** are popular for monitoring data and model drift, sending alerts when the model's performance drops below a threshold.
- **Benefits**: Helps maintain model accuracy, prevents issues before they affect end users, and reduces the need for constant manual monitoring.

9. Synthetic Data for Model Training and Testing

To overcome limitations related to data privacy, imbalance, or scarcity, companies are increasingly using **synthetic data** to train and test ML models. Synthetic data generation tools create artificial datasets that mimic real-world data without revealing sensitive information, making it valuable for industries like healthcare and finance.

- **Example**: **Gretel.ai** and **Synthea** provide synthetic data generation services for various industries, allowing teams to augment their data without risking privacy.
- **Benefits**: Enhances data diversity, reduces privacy concerns, and enables better training of models in data-scarce environments.

10. Edge MLOps for On-Device Learning

As IoT and edge devices grow, **Edge MLOps** is emerging as a trend where ML models are deployed on devices close to the data source, like mobile phones, industrial machines, or smart appliances. Edge MLOps focuses on managing these models and updating them directly on devices, reducing latency and making models responsive to local changes.

- **Example: TensorFlow Lite** and **AWS IoT Greengrass** support edge model deployment, allowing models to run inference on devices with limited computing power.
- **Benefits**: Reduces latency, minimizes cloud dependency, and enables ML in environments with limited connectivity.

11. Collaborative and Cross-Functional MLOps Workflows

As ML becomes central to business operations, **collaborative workflows** that integrate data engineering, software development, and data science are vital. Companies are adopting MLOps frameworks that support version control, issue tracking, and collaborative notebooks, enhancing teamwork and making ML development more agile.

- **Example**: Tools like **Weights & Biases**, **MLflow**, and **GitHub** facilitate collaboration across the ML lifecycle, enabling version control, experiment tracking, and artifact sharing.
- **Benefits**: Improves teamwork, accelerates iteration, and aligns development with business objectives.

Conclusion

The emerging trends in MLOps reflect a push toward greater automation, scalability, and reliability in ML systems. By embracing trends such as AutoML, data-centric approaches, federated learning, and real-time monitoring, organizations can build MLOps pipelines that are more adaptable, secure, and responsive to real-world conditions. This evolution of MLOps is essential to address the growing complexity and business demands of deploying machine learning at scale.

The Role of AI and Automation in MLOps

AI and automation play a crucial role in **MLOps (Machine Learning Operations)**, enabling more efficient, scalable, and resilient ML workflows. MLOps aims to streamline the end-to-end lifecycle of machine learning models—from development to deployment, monitoring, and updating. AI and automation significantly enhance these processes by reducing manual effort, improving accuracy, and allowing continuous integration and deployment of ML models. Here's how they contribute to MLOps:

1. Automated Data Processing and Feature Engineering

Data processing and feature engineering are essential steps in ML that require careful handling of large datasets and domain-specific transformations. Automation can streamline these tasks to ensure that data is high-quality, labeled accurately, and appropriately formatted for model training.

- **AI in Data Labeling and Augmentation**: AI-driven labeling tools (like Snorkel and Labelbox) use machine learning to assist in labeling large datasets, often leveraging NLP, computer vision, or domain-specific knowledge to reduce manual labeling.

- **Automated Feature Engineering**: Tools like **Featuretools** and **DataRobot** automate feature creation, extraction, and selection, helping ML practitioners create effective features without extensive manual tuning.

Benefit: Automation improves data consistency, reduces human error, and allows quicker iteration, making ML development more agile and data preparation more scalable.

2. Hyperparameter Optimization and Model Selection (AutoML)

Hyperparameter tuning and model selection are time-consuming tasks that can greatly impact model performance. **AutoML (Automated Machine Learning)** streamlines this by automating the process of experimenting with different models, hyperparameters, and feature engineering techniques.

- **Example Tools**: Google's **AutoML**, **H2O.ai**, **AutoKeras**, and **TPOT** perform tasks like model selection, hyperparameter optimization, and algorithm experimentation, helping data scientists find the best model and configuration for their data.
- **Automated Experiment Tracking**: Automation in experiment tracking (using tools like **MLflow, Weights & Biases**) enables better model comparisons, visualization, and tracking of each run's parameters and metrics.

Benefit: Faster experimentation with less human intervention, enabling rapid iteration and higher accuracy in model performance.

3. CI/CD Automation for Model Deployment

Continuous Integration and Continuous Deployment (CI/CD) pipelines in MLOps automate the testing, validation, and deployment of models, ensuring that new versions are integrated seamlessly into production.

- **Model Versioning and Testing**: Automation frameworks (e.g., **GitHub Actions**, **Jenkins**) facilitate version control and automatically test each model version to ensure quality before deployment.
- **Containerization and Orchestration: Docker** and **Kubernetes** enable automated container creation and management, making it easier to deploy models across various environments and scale model services as demand changes.

Benefit: Ensures consistent, reproducible, and scalable deployments, reducing deployment errors and increasing deployment frequency.

4. Automated Model Monitoring and Drift Detection

Once models are in production, continuous monitoring is essential to ensure they remain effective. AI and automation enable **model monitoring**, **drift detection**, and **anomaly detection** to track model performance in real-time and detect data drift or concept drift.

- **Automated Drift Detection**: Tools like **Evidently AI** and **WhyLabs** use machine learning to detect changes in data distribution, alerting teams when model retraining might be necessary.
- **Self-Healing Models**: Emerging AI-based monitoring solutions can trigger automatic retraining or fine-tuning of models when significant performance drops are detected.

Benefit: Automated monitoring prevents model degradation, helps maintain high model accuracy, and ensures timely response to changes in data patterns.

5. Model Retraining and Continuous Learning

Automation is critical in continuous learning, where models are retrained periodically or triggered by specific events (e.g., performance degradation, new data availability). This process is especially valuable for applications where data and user behavior change frequently.

- **Automated Retraining Pipelines**: CI/CD tools, along with scheduling frameworks (e.g., **Airflow**, **Kubeflow**), automate model retraining workflows, ensuring that updated models are deployed quickly.
- **Self-Adaptive Models**: With advancements in transfer learning and meta-learning, models can adjust to new data patterns with minimal retraining, reducing the need for complete retraining cycles.

Benefit: Models stay relevant and accurate without continuous manual intervention, saving time and resources and enhancing scalability.

6. Automated Infrastructure Management

Automation in infrastructure management is essential to handle the dynamic scaling needs of MLOps pipelines. As models require different computational resources during training, deployment, and monitoring, automated infrastructure management helps optimize resource allocation.

- **Auto-Scaling and Resource Optimization**: Cloud providers like AWS, GCP, and Azure offer managed services that automatically allocate compute resources based on model demand, optimizing costs and performance.
- **Serverless Architecture for Inference**: Tools like **AWS Lambda** and **Google Cloud Functions** enable automated scaling for model inference, where infrastructure scales automatically based on incoming requests.

Benefit: Reduces infrastructure costs, improves scalability, and allows MLOps pipelines to operate efficiently without manual configuration.

7. AI-Driven Decision Support and Explainability

Explainable AI (XAI) and interpretability tools help teams understand model predictions and provide transparency in decision-making. Automation in explainability ensures models in production can produce explanations without human intervention.

- **AI in Explainability**: Libraries like **SHAP** and **LIME** provide automated model explanations, which can be integrated into production for real-time interpretability.
- **Automated Decision-Making Systems**: For applications like fraud detection and recommendation systems, AI-driven decision-making processes offer real-time automated insights based on model predictions.

Benefit: Enhances model transparency, meets regulatory compliance, and builds trust in AI decisions by making predictions interpretable and explainable.

8. AI and Automation for Security and Compliance

As AI adoption increases, ensuring security and regulatory compliance has become a priority. Automation plays a key role in managing sensitive data, enforcing access controls, and tracking changes in models and data pipelines to meet compliance standards.

- **Automated Compliance Checks**: Tools like **Alteryx** and **Immuta** automate compliance workflows, ensuring data privacy and regulatory compliance by handling access controls and enforcing policies.
- **AI in Threat Detection**: AI-driven security solutions monitor MLOps pipelines for suspicious activities, helping prevent breaches, data leaks, and model tampering.

Benefit: Enhances security, reduces compliance risks, and allows organizations to confidently deploy AI in sensitive applications.

9. Collaborative AI and Workflow Automation in MLOps

AI-driven collaboration tools streamline workflows by automating experiment tracking, versioning, and collaborative documentation, making it easier for teams to work together.

- **AI-Powered Workflow Management**: Platforms like **Weights & Biases** and **DAGsHub** automate version control, experiment tracking, and reproducibility, enabling efficient collaboration across cross-functional teams.
- **Automated Reporting and Documentation**: Tools like **Neptune.ai** automatically generate reports based on training and testing outcomes, helping data science teams document model development for easy sharing.

Benefit: Improves productivity and collaboration, minimizes human error, and ensures consistency in model development and deployment.

Summary

The integration of AI and automation in MLOps makes machine learning pipelines more efficient, scalable, and adaptive, empowering organizations to build reliable AI systems that respond to real-world changes in near real-time. By automating data processing, model deployment, monitoring, retraining, and security, organizations can reduce human intervention, lower operational costs, and accelerate their AI initiatives. As MLOps evolves, automation will continue to enable more sophisticated, self-optimizing AI systems that drive innovation across industries.

Husn Ara

Next-Generation MLOps Tools and Techniques

Next-generation **MLOps tools and techniques** are advancing the way organizations manage machine learning models, making pipelines more efficient, resilient, and adaptable. These cutting-edge tools address complex challenges like multi-cloud deployments, real-time monitoring, data-centric workflows, and collaborative AI, bringing a more refined and dynamic approach to the MLOps lifecycle. Here's a breakdown of the emerging tools and techniques shaping the future of MLOps:

1. Data-Centric MLOps Tools

While traditional MLOps often focused on model-centric workflows, next-gen MLOps places data quality and consistency at the core. **Data-centric MLOps** tools emphasize ensuring that data is high-quality, unbiased, and representative to support robust ML models.

- **Examples**:
    - **Snorkel** and **Labelbox** for data labeling, allowing for efficient annotation and semi-automated data labeling.
    - **Tecton** and **Feast** as feature stores that facilitate feature engineering, versioning, and sharing across teams.
    - **Great Expectations** for data validation and profiling, allowing teams to automatically test data for anomalies or inconsistencies.
- **Benefits**: Ensures high-quality data, reduces the risk of data drift, and streamlines data preparation for ML models, ultimately enhancing model accuracy and consistency.

2. Multi-Cloud and Hybrid MLOps Platforms

Multi-cloud and hybrid infrastructures allow organizations to deploy and scale models across different cloud providers or on-

345

premises environments. These platforms are designed to prevent vendor lock-in and provide flexibility and resiliency.

- **Examples**:
    - ○ **KubeFlow** and **MLflow** enable model deployment and tracking across multiple cloud platforms like AWS, GCP, and Azure, allowing for hybrid and multi-cloud MLOps.
    - ○ **Seldon Core** for Kubernetes-based model deployment and management, which supports scalable multi-cloud and hybrid setups.
    - ○ **DVC (Data Version Control)** and **Pachyderm** facilitate multi-cloud data management with version control.
- **Benefits**: Provides flexibility, avoids vendor lock-in, and enables seamless scalability and fault tolerance across diverse infrastructure setups.

3. Real-Time Monitoring and Observability

Real-time model monitoring and observability tools are crucial to detect performance degradation, data drift, and other issues that may impact model performance in production.

- **Examples**:
    - ○ **Evidently AI** and **WhyLabs** for automated model monitoring, tracking data drift, and generating alerts.
    - ○ **Arize AI** offers end-to-end model observability, helping monitor and troubleshoot models in production.
    - ○ **Monte Carlo** provides data observability by detecting data quality issues in real-time.
- **Benefits**: Ensures model reliability, reduces downtime, and supports continuous optimization by proactively identifying issues as they arise.

4. Edge and Federated MLOps

As edge computing grows, tools are emerging to support the deployment of models on edge devices and across decentralized data sources using federated learning. This is particularly relevant for privacy-sensitive applications and real-time decision-making at the edge.

- **Examples**:
    - **TensorFlow Lite** and **AWS IoT Greengrass** for deploying lightweight ML models on edge devices.
    - **PySyft** and **Federated TensorFlow** for federated learning, allowing model training across devices without centralizing sensitive data.
    - **NVIDIA Fleet Command** provides orchestration and management of models at the edge, enabling large-scale edge deployments.
- **Benefits**: Enhances privacy, reduces latency, and enables AI capabilities in environments with limited connectivity, such as IoT and remote monitoring systems.

5. Automated Model Re-training and Adaptive Learning

Adaptive learning and automated re-training pipelines are emerging as vital components of next-gen MLOps. These pipelines leverage continuous learning frameworks to enable models to update as new data becomes available.

- **Examples**:
    - **Airflow** and **Kubeflow Pipelines** enable automated re-training workflows, triggering training jobs based on data drift or performance degradation.
    - **Continual** is a platform for continuous learning in MLOps, automating re-training and deployment.
    - **Evidently AI** offers drift detection and can trigger re-training workflows to keep models up-to-date.
- **Benefits**: Ensures models remain relevant, responsive to new data patterns, and minimizes human intervention for ongoing model maintenance.

6. Explainability and Interpretability Tools

Explainable AI (XAI) tools are essential for organizations looking to implement responsible AI practices, providing insights into model predictions to make them transparent and accountable.

- **Examples**:
  - **SHAP** and **LIME** for post-hoc model interpretability, allowing teams to explain individual predictions.
  - **Alibi Explain** and **Explainable Boosting Machine (EBM)** provide interpretable models, helping data scientists understand feature importance and decision boundaries.
  - **Fiddler AI** and **TruEra** provide explainability as a service, enabling transparency and regulatory compliance in AI-driven systems.
- **Benefits**: Increases trust in model predictions, ensures compliance with regulatory standards, and supports ethical AI practices in high-stakes applications like healthcare and finance.

7. Collaborative MLOps Platforms and Experiment Tracking

Collaborative tools in MLOps foster teamwork across data scientists, ML engineers, and business stakeholders by automating experiment tracking, versioning, and reporting.

- **Examples**:
  - **Weights & Biases**, **Neptune.ai**, and **Comet** offer experiment tracking and artifact management, helping teams visualize, compare, and share model training results.
  - **DAGsHub** is a Git-based collaboration tool that combines version control, experiment tracking, and data management in one platform.
  - **MLflow** enables centralized tracking and comparison of experiments, simplifying the model selection process.

- **Benefits**: Enhances productivity, allows reproducibility, and makes collaboration seamless across distributed teams working on ML projects.

8. Synthetic Data Generation for Model Training

Synthetic data generation addresses challenges related to data privacy, data scarcity, or imbalanced datasets. These tools create artificial data that closely resembles real-world data without compromising sensitive information.

- **Examples**:
  - **Gretel.ai** and **Synthea** generate synthetic datasets for training ML models in industries with stringent data privacy requirements, like healthcare and finance.
  - **Datagen** and **DataSynthesizer** produce synthetic data for image and NLP applications, enabling data augmentation and training diversity.
  - **Mostly AI** creates synthetic data that balances data attributes to combat bias in model training.
- **Benefits**: Overcomes data scarcity, ensures data privacy, and provides balanced datasets to reduce bias in model training.

9. Automated Security and Compliance in MLOps

As ML applications expand into sensitive domains, security and compliance automation are key. These tools monitor for threats, enforce access controls, and ensure adherence to regulatory standards.

- **Examples**:
  - **Immuta** and **Alteryx** for automated compliance workflows, helping organizations comply with data privacy regulations like GDPR.
  - **AI Fairness 360 (AIF360)** by IBM for bias detection and mitigation, providing pre- and post-processing algorithms to promote fairness.

- o **Snyk** for detecting vulnerabilities in ML codebases and dependencies, ensuring that models are secure against potential attacks.
- **Benefits**: Protects sensitive data, mitigates compliance risks, and allows organizations to deploy ML systems securely and responsibly.

10. Self-Service MLOps Platforms and No-Code/Low-Code Interfaces

Self-service MLOps platforms are increasingly popular for enabling business analysts and non-technical users to create, deploy, and manage ML models with minimal coding.

- **Examples**:
  - o **DataRobot** and **H2O.ai** offer no-code/low-code platforms that allow non-experts to build and deploy ML models.
  - o **RapidMiner** and **Azure ML Designer** provide drag-and-drop interfaces for model creation and deployment, reducing the technical barrier to entry.
  - o **Akkio** and **Peltarion** offer end-to-end MLOps with no-code interfaces, allowing users to focus on business outcomes rather than model implementation details.
- **Benefits**: Democratizes ML, reduces dependency on data science expertise, and accelerates model deployment for business applications.

11. Serverless MLOps and Function-as-a-Service (FaaS)

Serverless MLOps simplifies model deployment by abstracting infrastructure management, allowing teams to focus on development and deployment without managing servers.

- **Examples**:
  - o **AWS Lambda** and **Google Cloud Functions** for serverless model inference, enabling auto-scaling based on incoming requests.

- o **Nimbella** and **Zappa** for deploying serverless applications, supporting MLOps workflows that dynamically adjust resources according to demand.
- o **MLRun** provides serverless orchestration for machine learning, managing workflows and scaling resources automatically.
- **Benefits**: Reduces infrastructure costs, provides elastic scaling, and supports cost-effective model serving for variable workloads.

Summary

Next-generation MLOps tools and techniques are designed to handle the growing complexity of ML workflows, catering to diverse infrastructure setups, ensuring data quality, and supporting continuous model monitoring and adaptive learning. By adopting these innovations, organizations can deploy robust, reliable, and explainable models that respond dynamically to real-world changes and align with regulatory, ethical, and privacy standards. This new wave of MLOps enables faster, smarter, and more accessible AI solutions for various industries.

Appendix

Glossary of Key MLOps Terms

MLOps (Machine Learning Operations) is a set of practices that unifies machine learning (ML) system development and operations (Ops). It aims to automate the entire ML lifecycle, from data collection and preparation to model deployment, monitoring, and maintenance. Below is a glossary of key MLOps terms to help you understand this field better.

A

- **Accuracy**: A performance metric that measures the proportion of correct predictions made by the model compared to the total predictions. Often used in classification tasks.
- **API (Application Programming Interface)**: A set of protocols that allows different software systems to communicate with each other. In MLOps, APIs are often used to expose machine learning models for inference.
- **Artifact**: Any file or object produced during an ML workflow. Common artifacts include models, datasets, logs, and visualizations.
- **AutoML (Automated Machine Learning)**: A set of tools and techniques that automates the process of model

selection, hyperparameter tuning, and feature engineering, allowing non-experts to create models.

B

- **Batch Processing**: A method where data is processed in chunks, typically for training models in a non-real-time fashion. This is useful for large datasets.
- **Bayesian Optimization**: A probabilistic model-based optimization technique used for hyperparameter tuning. It is more efficient than grid search for complex hyperparameter spaces.

C

- **CI/CD (Continuous Integration / Continuous Deployment)**: A set of practices in software engineering that ensures code changes are automatically tested and deployed. In MLOps, it refers to automating the deployment of machine learning models.
- **Checkpointing**: Saving the state of a machine learning model or training process at a specific point in time, allowing you to resume training from that point.
- **Concept Drift**: A phenomenon where the statistical properties of the target variable change over time, which may affect model performance.
- **Containerization**: The practice of packaging machine learning models and environments (including libraries and dependencies) into containers (like Docker) for easy deployment.

D

- **Data Drift**: A shift in the distribution of input data over time, which can degrade model performance. Monitoring for data drift is crucial for maintaining model accuracy in production.
- **Data Versioning**: The practice of keeping track of changes to datasets over time. Tools like **DVC** (Data Version Control) help manage and version datasets, ensuring reproducibility.

- **Deployment Pipeline**: An automated pipeline for deploying machine learning models to production, ensuring smooth integration of newly trained models.

E

- **Experiment Tracking**: The practice of logging and organizing experiments, including hyperparameters, datasets, models, and performance metrics. Tools like **MLflow** and **Weights & Biases** support this functionality.
- **Environment Management**: The process of managing software environments, including libraries, frameworks, and dependencies, to ensure reproducibility across experiments. Tools like **Conda** and **Docker** are often used.

F

- **Feature Engineering**: The process of selecting, modifying, or creating new features from raw data to improve the performance of a machine learning model.
- **Feature Store**: A centralized repository that stores and manages features for machine learning models, ensuring consistency and reusability across teams and projects.
- **F1 Score**: A metric that combines precision and recall into a single score, balancing both false positives and false negatives. It is commonly used in classification tasks with imbalanced datasets.

G

- **Grid Search**: A hyperparameter optimization technique where all possible combinations of hyperparameters are tested exhaustively. It can be computationally expensive but guarantees finding the best combination.
- **GPU (Graphics Processing Unit)**: A hardware component used to accelerate computations, particularly beneficial in deep learning tasks that require high computational power.

H

- **Hyperparameter Tuning**: The process of finding the optimal set of hyperparameters (e.g., learning rate, batch size) that result in the best model performance. Techniques include grid search, random search, and Bayesian optimization.
- **Hyperparameter**: A parameter whose value is set before the model training process. Examples include the number of trees in a random forest or the learning rate in gradient descent.

I

- **Inference**: The process of using a trained machine learning model to make predictions on new data.
- **Integrated Development Environment (IDE)**: A software application that provides comprehensive tools for software development. In MLOps, common IDEs include **VSCode**, **PyCharm**, and **Jupyter Notebooks**.
- **Input Pipeline**: A system for feeding data into a machine learning model, ensuring that data is preprocessed and ready for model training or inference.

J

- **Jupyter Notebooks**: An open-source web application that allows you to create and share documents that include live code, equations, visualizations, and narrative text. It is often used in data science and machine learning for experimentation and prototyping.

K

- **Kubeflow**: An open-source platform for deploying, monitoring, and managing machine learning models in Kubernetes environments. It provides tools for automating ML workflows.
- **Kubernetes**: A container orchestration platform used to manage and deploy containerized applications at scale.

In MLOps, Kubernetes helps with the deployment and scaling of ML models in production.

L

- **Logging**: The process of recording information about model training, performance, and errors. Logging is essential for debugging and monitoring machine learning systems.
- **Lifecycle Management**: The process of managing the various stages of a machine learning model, including data collection, model training, deployment, and maintenance.

M

- **Model Drift**: A scenario where a deployed model's performance degrades over time due to changes in the underlying data or environment.
- **Model Monitoring**: The practice of continuously tracking a model's performance in production to detect issues like model drift, data drift, or performance degradation.
- **MLflow**: An open-source platform to manage the end-to-end lifecycle of machine learning models, including experiment tracking, model versioning, and deployment.

N

- **Neural Networks**: A type of machine learning model inspired by the structure of the human brain. It is used extensively in deep learning for tasks like image recognition and natural language processing.
- **NLP (Natural Language Processing)**: A field of AI that focuses on enabling machines to understand, interpret, and generate human language.

P

- **Pipeline**: A set of automated steps that define the end-to-end process of building, training, and deploying a machine learning model.
- **Preprocessing**: The set of operations performed on raw data to clean and transform it into a format suitable for training machine learning models.
- **Precision**: A metric that measures the accuracy of positive predictions. It is the ratio of true positives to all predicted positives.

R

- **Reproducibility**: The ability to replicate an experiment or model by following the same steps with the same code, data, and environment.
- **Random Search**: A hyperparameter tuning technique where random combinations of hyperparameters are sampled from a predefined search space.

S

- **Scalability**: The ability of a system or application to handle a growing amount of work or data, or to be capable of being expanded to accommodate that growth.
- **SaaS (Software as a Service)**: A cloud-based service model where software applications, including machine learning platforms, are delivered over the internet.
- **Shapley Values**: A technique from game theory used to explain the contribution of each feature to the model's predictions.

T

- **TensorFlow**: An open-source machine learning framework developed by Google, widely used for training and deploying deep learning models.
- **Tuning**: The process of adjusting hyperparameters or other model configurations to improve the model's performance.

- **Training**: The process of teaching a machine learning model by feeding it labeled data and adjusting its parameters to minimize errors.

U

- **User Interface (UI)**: The visual and interactive components of a software application, such as dashboards and control panels, used for monitoring models or managing experiments in MLOps.

V

- **Versioning**: The practice of assigning unique identifiers to different versions of data, models, and code to keep track of changes over time.
- **Validation Set**: A subset of the dataset used to evaluate the performance of a model during training to prevent overfitting.

W

- **Weights & Biases (W&B)**: A tool for experiment tracking, model management, and visualization in machine learning workflows.
- **Webhooks**: A method used to trigger automated actions when a specific event occurs, often used for notifying teams when experiments are completed or models are deployed.

This glossary serves as an overview of the most commonly used terms in MLOps. Understanding these terms is crucial for building efficient, scalable, and reproducible machine learning systems.

Recommended Tools and Resources for MLOps

MLOps (Machine Learning Operations) integrates machine learning into the software engineering practices to ensure reproducibility, scalability, and automated deployment of models. To effectively implement MLOps, various tools and resources are available that cover different stages of the machine learning lifecycle, from experimentation to deployment and monitoring. Here's a comprehensive list of recommended tools and resources for MLOps:

1. Experiment Tracking and Management

- **MLflow**: An open-source platform for managing the end-to-end machine learning lifecycle, including experimentation, reproducibility, and deployment.
  - o **Features**: Experiment tracking, model versioning, artifact storage, and model deployment.
  - o **Website**: MLflow
- **Weights & Biases (W&B)**: A popular tool for experiment tracking, visualization, and collaboration, making it easier to track hyperparameters, metrics, and models.
  - o **Features**: Experiment tracking, model management, hyperparameter optimization, and team collaboration.
  - o **Website**: Weights & Biases
- **Comet.ml**: A platform for managing experiments, models, datasets, and monitoring ML projects in real time.
  - o **Features**: Tracking experiments, version control for models, and collaboration.
  - o **Website**: Comet.ml
- **DVC (Data Version Control)**: An open-source tool that helps with version control for data and models, enabling reproducible experiments in a collaborative environment.
  - o **Features**: Data and model versioning, integration with Git, and pipeline management.
  - o **Website**: DVC

2. Model Deployment and Monitoring

- **TensorFlow Extended (TFX)**: A production-ready machine learning platform that helps build and deploy end-to-end machine learning pipelines.
  - o **Features**: Data validation, transformation, model training, model deployment, and monitoring.
  - o **Website**: TensorFlow Extended
- **Kubeflow**: An open-source platform for deploying and managing machine learning workflows on Kubernetes, helping automate deployment, scaling, and monitoring of models.
  - o **Features**: Model serving, training, hyperparameter tuning, and pipeline orchestration.
  - o **Website**: Kubeflow
- **Seldon**: A machine learning deployment platform that helps you deploy, monitor, and manage machine learning models in production.
  - o **Features**: Model deployment, A/B testing, canary deployments, and monitoring.
  - o **Website**: Seldon
- **MLflow** (again): In addition to experiment tracking, MLflow also offers **model deployment** via its mlflow models API, making it versatile in both development and production.
  - o **Website**: MLflow Deployment
- **Prometheus & Grafana**: For monitoring the performance of machine learning models in production, Prometheus collects metrics, and Grafana provides real-time dashboards for visualization.
  - o **Website**: Prometheus, Grafana

3. Hyperparameter Optimization

- **Optuna**: An open-source hyperparameter optimization framework that uses an efficient search algorithm for automatic hyperparameter tuning.
  - o **Features**: Hyperparameter optimization, pruning, and integration with ML frameworks like TensorFlow, PyTorch, and scikit-learn.
  - o **Website**: Optuna

- **Ray Tune**: A scalable and efficient hyperparameter optimization library built on top of Ray. It supports both distributed and asynchronous optimization.
  - o **Features**: Parallel hyperparameter tuning, integration with popular machine learning frameworks.
  - o **Website**: Ray Tune
- **Hyperopt**: A popular library for hyperparameter optimization using algorithms like random search, grid search, and Bayesian optimization.
  - o **Features**: Supports distributed computing for optimization tasks.
  - o **Website**: Hyperopt

4. Continuous Integration/Continuous Deployment (CI/CD)

- **Jenkins**: A widely used open-source automation server that supports CI/CD pipelines for automating testing and deployment, including for machine learning workflows.
  - o **Features**: Automation, pipeline orchestration, plugin integrations.
  - o **Website**: Jenkins
- **GitLab CI/CD**: GitLab's integrated CI/CD tools provide a complete DevOps lifecycle management for continuous deployment and integration of machine learning models.
  - o **Features**: Automated pipeline management, version control integration.
  - o **Website**: GitLab CI/CD
- **CircleCI**: A cloud-based CI/CD tool that offers automation for testing, building, and deploying machine learning models.
  - o **Features**: Continuous integration and delivery, integration with ML frameworks.
  - o **Website**: CircleCI

5. Containerization and Virtualization

- **Docker**: A containerization platform that helps package machine learning models and their dependencies into isolated environments for easier deployment.

- o **Features**: Environment consistency, portability, and scaling.
  - o **Website**: Docker
- **Kubernetes**: An open-source container orchestration platform for automating the deployment, scaling, and management of containerized applications, including ML models.
  - o **Features**: Scaling, self-healing, container orchestration.
  - o **Website**: Kubernetes
- **Helm**: A package manager for Kubernetes that helps deploy complex applications like machine learning models and data pipelines on Kubernetes clusters.
  - o **Features**: Managing Kubernetes packages, automating deployment.
  - o **Website**: Helm

6. Data Management and Feature Engineering

- **Apache Kafka**: A distributed event streaming platform for building real-time data pipelines, which is crucial for managing real-time data flows into machine learning models.
  - o **Features**: Real-time data processing, message queues, data streaming.
  - o **Website**: Apache Kafka
- **FeatureStore**: A feature management and storage system designed to manage features used in machine learning models. Examples include **Feast** (open-source) and **Tecton** (enterprise-grade).
  - o **Website**: Feast, Tecton
- **Snowflake**: A cloud data platform that provides an integrated data warehouse, which can be used for large-scale data processing and analytics in MLOps.
  - o **Features**: Data warehousing, real-time analytics, and scalability.
  - o **Website**: Snowflake

7. Model Interpretability and Explainability

- **SHAP (SHapley Additive exPlanations)**: A popular library for model interpretability, SHAP provides a unified approach to explaining machine learning models based on Shapley values.

- o **Features**: Model explainability, feature importance analysis.
- o **Website**: SHAP
- **LIME (Local Interpretable Model-agnostic Explanations)**: A library for model interpretability that provides explanations by approximating a model's predictions with a simpler interpretable model.
  - o **Features**: Local interpretability, black-box model explanation.
  - o **Website**: LIME

8. Cloud-Based MLOps Platforms

- **Amazon SageMaker**: A fully managed service by AWS for building, training, and deploying machine learning models at scale.
  - o **Features**: Model training, hosting, monitoring, and versioning.
  - o **Website**: Amazon SageMaker
- **Google AI Platform**: A suite of tools by Google Cloud for developing, deploying, and managing machine learning models.
  - o **Features**: Managed training, hyperparameter tuning, model monitoring.
  - o **Website**: Google AI Platform
- **Azure Machine Learning**: A fully managed cloud service by Microsoft for building, training, and deploying machine learning models.
  - o **Features**: Automated ML, hyperparameter tuning, model monitoring.
  - o **Website**: Azure Machine Learning

9. Documentation and Knowledge Sharing

- **Sphinx**: A documentation generator for Python projects, often used to create project documentation, including MLOps pipelines and experiment details.
  - o **Website**: Sphinx

- **Notion**: A collaboration tool for organizing and documenting machine learning projects, workflows, and experiments in a flexible format.
  - ○ **Website**: Notion
- **Confluence**: A collaboration platform that can be used to create, share, and collaborate on project documentation and knowledge bases.
  - ○ **Website**: Confluence

These tools help ensure that MLOps practices can be effectively implemented, supporting various aspects of the machine learning lifecycle including experimentation, deployment, monitoring, scaling, and collaboration. The choice of tools depends on your team's specific requirements, existing infrastructure, and project goals.

Further Reading and References for MLOps

To deepen your understanding of MLOps (Machine Learning Operations) and stay updated on the latest developments, it's helpful to explore various books, research papers, blogs, online courses, and open-source resources. Below are some curated recommendations for further reading and exploration in the field of MLOps.

Books

1. **"Building Machine Learning Pipelines" by Hannes Hapke and Catherine Nelson**
   - ○ **Overview**: This book focuses on creating robust and scalable machine learning pipelines using modern tools and techniques. It covers the entire ML lifecycle, from data ingestion to model deployment, with practical examples.
   - ○ **Link**: Building Machine Learning Pipelines
2. **"Machine Learning Engineering" by Andriy Burkov**

o **Overview**: A comprehensive guide to the intersection of machine learning and software engineering. It explores the skills required to build production-ready machine learning systems.
o **Link**: Machine Learning Engineering
3. **"Data Science at Scale with Python and Dask" by Thomas Wiecki**
   o **Overview**: This book delves into scaling machine learning models using the Dask library. It covers parallel computing, distributed data processing, and MLOps for large datasets and model management.
   o **Link**: Data Science at Scale with Python and Dask
4. **"Practical MLOps: Operationalizing Machine Learning Models" by Noah Gift and Alfredo Deza**
   o **Overview**: Focuses on operationalizing machine learning models, automating workflows, and deploying machine learning systems in production.
   o **Link**: Practical MLOps

Research Papers and Articles

1. **"MLOps: Continuous Delivery and Automation Pipelines in Machine Learning"**
   o **Overview**: This paper presents MLOps as a set of practices and technologies to integrate ML models into software systems, detailing the challenges and solutions in model deployment and monitoring.
   o **Link**: MLOps Paper
2. **"The ML Ops Landscape" by C. N. K. R. Sathish**
   o **Overview**: This research explores various practices and technologies related to MLOps, including the tools for managing machine learning models in production environments.
   o **Link**: ML Ops Landscape
3. **"Machine Learning Engineering for Production (MLOps)" by Andrew Ng (DeepLearning.AI)**
   o **Overview**: A short research paper detailing the methodology, techniques, and practices for

taking machine learning models from experimentation to production.
  o **Link**: Machine Learning Engineering for Production

Online Courses

1. **"MLOps Fundamentals" by Google Cloud**
   o **Overview**: A free course by Google Cloud that introduces key concepts in MLOps, including model lifecycle management, automation, and versioning.
   o **Link**: MLOps Fundamentals
2. **"Machine Learning Engineering for Production (MLOps)" by Andrew Ng (DeepLearning.AI)**
   o **Overview**: A highly recommended course that provides an in-depth understanding of how to deploy machine learning models in real-world environments using MLOps practices.
   o **Link**: Machine Learning Engineering for Production
3. **"Practical MLOps" by Coursera (offered by University of California, Berkeley)**
   o **Overview**: This course covers the full end-to-end process of machine learning in production, including experimentation, deployment, monitoring, and model management.
   o **Link**: Practical MLOps Course
4. **"Introduction to MLOps" by Microsoft**
   o **Overview**: Learn about the importance of MLOps in machine learning projects and how to set up automation, pipelines, and monitoring systems for scalable ML deployments.
   o **Link**: Introduction to MLOps

Blogs and Websites

1. **MLOps Community Blog**
   o **Overview**: A hub for everything related to MLOps, offering articles, case studies, and best practices from professionals in the field.
   o **Link**: MLOps Community

2. **Google Cloud Blog: MLOps**
   o **Overview**: Insights on best practices, tools, and real-world examples of MLOps from Google Cloud's engineers.
   o **Link**: Google Cloud Blog - MLOps
3. **Microsoft Azure Blog: MLOps**
   o **Overview**: Microsoft's blog offering insights and practical guides on implementing MLOps practices on Azure, including model deployment, monitoring, and lifecycle management.
   o **Link**: Microsoft Azure Blog - MLOps
4. **Towards Data Science: MLOps**
   o **Overview**: A popular Medium publication where data science and machine learning professionals share their insights into MLOps, model monitoring, deployment, and scaling.
   o **Link**: Towards Data Science - MLOps

Open Source Tools and Repositories

1. **Kubeflow**
   o **Overview**: An open-source platform for managing ML workflows, Kubeflow supports the entire machine learning pipeline, including model deployment and monitoring.
   o **Link**: Kubeflow GitHub
2. **MLflow**
   o **Overview**: A leading open-source platform for managing the complete machine learning lifecycle, including experiment tracking, model deployment, and monitoring.
   o **Link**: MLflow GitHub
3. **DVC (Data Version Control)**
   o **Overview**: DVC is an open-source version control system for managing machine learning models, data, and experiments. It integrates with Git and can handle large datasets.
   o **Link**: DVC GitHub
4. **Seldon**
   o **Overview**: An open-source platform for deploying, monitoring, and managing machine learning models in production. It is particularly useful for model versioning and A/B testing.

o **Link**: Seldon GitHub

Conferences and Events

1. **MLOps World Conference**
   o **Overview**: An annual conference that brings together MLOps practitioners, data scientists, and engineers to discuss the latest tools, trends, and challenges in machine learning operations.
   o **Link**: MLOps World
2. **The AI Summit (Global)**
   o **Overview**: A global event series focused on artificial intelligence, including MLOps. The summit brings together AI leaders to discuss innovation, deployment, and challenges.
   o **Link**: The AI Summit
3. **KubeCon + CloudNativeCon**
   o **Overview**: A key conference for cloud-native technologies, including Kubernetes, which plays a significant role in deploying machine learning models in production environments.
   o **Link**: KubeCon + CloudNativeCon

Podcasts

1. **The MLOps Podcast**
   o **Overview**: A podcast that focuses on MLOps topics such as model deployment, pipeline management, monitoring, and scalability. It features interviews with industry experts.
   o **Link**: The MLOps Podcast
2. **Data Skeptic: MLOps Series**
   o **Overview**: This podcast series covers the practical and technical aspects of MLOps, including real-world challenges and solutions in deploying machine learning models.
   o **Link**: Data Skeptic
3. **The AI Alignment Podcast**
   o **Overview**: While not specifically about MLOps, this podcast delves into the technical challenges of deploying AI systems and provides valuable

context for ethical and technical considerations in AI deployments.

- o **Link**: AI Alignment Podcast

These resources should provide you with a well-rounded foundation in MLOps, helping you stay current with best practices, tools, and techniques in the rapidly evolving field of machine learning operations.

www.ingramcontent.com/pod-product-compliance
Lightning Source LLC
LaVergne TN
LVHW051427050326
832903LV00030BD/2956